THE AGE OF ABSOLUTISM

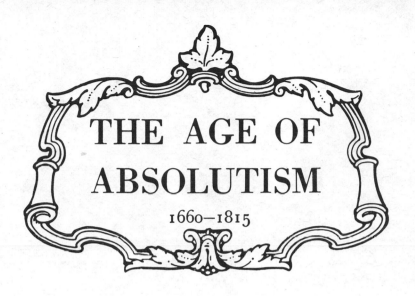

THE AGE OF ABSOLUTISM

1660–1815

MAX BELOFF

HARPER TORCHBOOKS ❧ THE ACADEMY LIBRARY

HARPER & ROW, PUBLISHERS · NEW YORK

to

P. D . W.

THE AGE OF ABSOLUTISM,
1660-1815

Printed in the United States of America

This book was originally published in the History series of the Hutchinson University Library, edited by Sir Maurice Powicke, in 1954, and is reprinted by arrangement with Hutchinson & Co., Ltd., London.

First HARPER TORCHBOOK edition published 1962

CONTENTS

MAPS

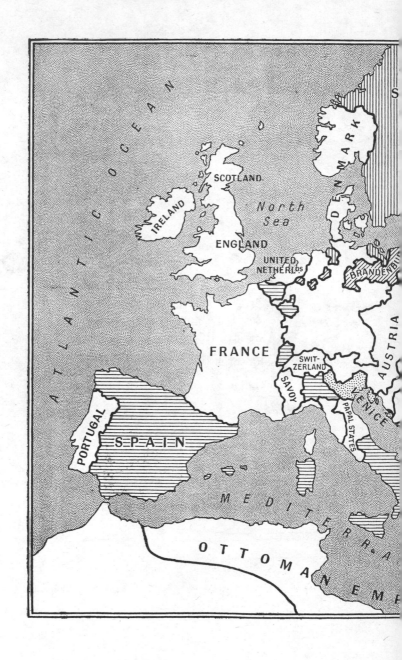

THE GREAT POWERS
OF EUROPE : 1660

Brandenburg – Prussia
Swedish Empire
Spanish　　"
Venice

0　　　200　　　400 MILES

DEN

E.PRUSSIA

POLAND

R U S S I A

Caspian Sea

Black Sea

O T T O M A N

E M P I R E

A N   S E A

"GEOGRAPHIA" LTD.

PREFACE

THE suggestion that I might write an essay on the Age of Absolutism was made to me by Sir Maurice Powicke a number of years ago at a time when I was working on the American Revolution. But for his constant and kindly encouragement, I would long ago have abandoned the attempt, deterred by the difficulty of the theme and the doubts which were bound to arise as to the method of treatment. What follows is by no means to be thought of as a compendium of eighteenth-century European history. I have tried instead to emphasize some elements in the society and politics of the period which appear to be of most consequence from the point of view of those whose interest in history is the pragmatic one of trying to understand their own times. To look at a political system from the point of view of the revolution which brought it to an end may seem needlessly perverse: in the space allotted to me, it has certainly meant omitting much which a full portrait of the age would demand. I can only hope that the starkness of outline which such selectivity imposes will help to reveal in their due importance certain aspects of the period which a fuller and more conventional treatment might fail sufficiently to emphasize. I am deeply indebted to Mr. John Bromley, Fellow of Keble College, for his constructive reading of the proofs. I am also grateful to Miss Molly Rubin of St. Hilda's College for assistance with the index.

M.B.

Oxford,
October 1953.

CHAPTER I

THE AGE DEFINED

THE choice of an historical period as the subject of a book is itself an intellectual commitment, since the notion of period is arbitrarily imposed upon a continuous development. But it is one of the choices that have to be made, if history is to be intelligible. The problem has often been avoided by recourse to the habit of thinking in centuries—a habit that comes naturally to people brought up on a decimal system of numerals. So pervasive is this tendency that some historians have written as though the centuries themselves were the subject of their inquiry, and have attempted to define an "eighteenth century" or "nineteenth century" attitude or style. The phrase *fin de siècle* meaning decadent is used about writers of the 1890s in oblivion of the fact that the 1790s were for a whole generation of poets an era of rebirth and renewal, when "to be young was very heaven".

Equally dangerous are terms that carry in themselves the description of an age and are so broad and general that no precise chronological limits can reasonably be assigned to them. Anyone who is aware of the prolonged and sometimes acrimonious discussions as to when the "Renaissance" took place or as to what centuries fall within the "Dark Ages", can see into what purely verbal entanglements one is ensnared.

The period 1660–1815 designated here as the "Age of Absolutism" can easily be assailed as providing a framework that helps to conceal as many important lines of demarcation as it suggests. And there is much truth in this argument.

The historian whose main interests lie in economic life would point out, for instance, that the first half of the eighteenth century saw little change in the techniques of production or in the economic relations resulting from them. In the latter half of the century, however, there took place the first of those major changes that are usually classed together as the "indus-

11

trial revolution", so that at the end of our period the "railway age" with all that the phrase implies is almost upon us. The new science of the demographers has noted that it is at some point within the period probably about 1750 that there begins a considerable acceleration in the rate at which the population of Europe increased, after long centuries of relative stability. We may roughly estimate they tell us, the population of Europe in 1700 as 118,500,000, in 1750 as 140,000,000 and in 1800 as 187,000,000. And they are no doubt right in asserting that such a change of which the causes are still obscure, had profound intellectual as well as social effects, so that the middle of the eighteenth century becomes the real turning point.

Yet to those who argue in this way, it is possible to answer that the change in the economic structure and in mortality rates rested on technical developments that were themselves the product of major theoretical advances in the natural sciences, and that these were on their way to being accomplished in the middle of the seventeenth century. This scientific revolution that we may try to locate within the familiar history of this island by thinking of the discussions leading to the formation of the Royal Society as taking place during the turmoil of our own Interregnum in the 1650s, increasingly appears to historians as of at least equal importance with the revival of classical studies in Italy two centuries earlier. Nor of course was the development in technique, in the control and utilization by man of natural resources, the only result of this scientific revolution. This was one of the ways in which it reacted upon the problems of society and government.

For only the relative peace and stability conferred upon the countries of western Europe by the strong governments of the early part of the "Age of Absolutism" could provide the social atmosphere within which the sciences could flourish, and economic life with them. On the other hand the social impact of economic advance whose benefits were necessarily unevenly distributed as between one class or group and another, presented the biggest of the problems faced by the legislator and administrator. In a relatively static society the prescriptions of monarchical absolutism might have worked better and its institutions have proved more durable. And furthermore, this new pre-occupation with mathematics was an essential element in the novel governmental attitudes of the period. In the second half of the seventeenth century men like Sir William Petty in England and Vauban in France, began to turn to the possibility of using the statistical method for the study and regulation of society, for purposes more far-reaching and subtle than the simple inquiries into individual and local taxable capacity that inspired Domesday Book and the other surveys of the Middle Ages.

One can find precedents indeed, for the attention paid by Louis XIV's great minister Colbert to the collection and analysis of statistics. But it was during his period of office that the regularity and continuity of the practice was first established. In an absolute monarchy the purpose of statistical inquiries—such as those in the 1690s by the Intendants (chief administrative officers) of the thirty-two "generalities" into which France was divided for governmental purposes—was still to aid the monarchy in its task, and their findings were consequently regarded as State secrets, as they continued to be in absolutist Russia well into the nineteenth century. The Swiss banker Necker, who was the French minister of finance in the period immediately before the Revolution was one of the earliest advocates of the publication, and interchange, of statistical information.

Because of the popular belief that such knowledge could benefit only the government and not the subject, the collection of this information was unpopular. A bill for a census in Great Britain was rejected in 1753 as dangerous to the liberties of the subject. And although there were partial and inaccurate attempts at a census in countries as far apart as Spain and Sweden, and in various other lands, it was necessary in this field of government as in others, to await the coming of democracy to do what the old absolutism had proved too weak to accomplish. The first modern census was that of the United States in 1790; the French Constituent Assembly ordered one in 1791 but it was not carried out properly; and the first real census in France as in Britain dates from 1801.

This relative inaccessibility of the necessary information— even though compensated for to some extent, by non-official investigations such as the celebrated inquiry of Gregory King into the population and wealth of England in the reign of William III—may help to explain why the theoretical apparatus of economics in its modern sense took so long to develop despite the long history (going back at least to the fifteenth century) of intellectual inquiry into isolated economic phenomena such as foreign exchange rates.

The final major impact of the scientific revolution—and in the long run, the most decisive and dramatic—is the secularization of society and thought that it helped to promote. The period might be regarded from this point of view as an age of comparative scepticism and toleration—at least where the educated strata of society were concerned—between the fierce wars of religion following the Protestant Reformation and the conflicts of the "secular religions" of our day which are in large part a legacy of the French Revolution. The impact of the scientific revolution was only one of the factors in the destruction of the old certainties. The development of a new critical approach to history—itself paradoxically the work of devout churchmen such as the French Benedictines of St. Maur—was another. And still more important was the widening of geographical horizons leading to an amateur but influential dabbling in what would now be described as comparative social anthropology (though the terms were then unknown) and a consequent weakening of the notion that civilization itself was identical with what had been transmitted to the moderns from Jerusalem, Athens and ancient Rome.

It was because they diffused this new scepticism rather than because they themselves were pioneers of the scientific spirit that the French "philosophes" of the eighteenth century retain their great rôle in European history. A Fontenelle was as necessary from this point of view, as a Newton from the other. And it was the diffusion of scepticism that made it impossible, at least in the areas profoundly touched by the "enlightenment", for political absolutism to rely upon divine authority. It was compelled to argue its case in the human arena, as Hobbes a forerunner had argued it in seventeenth-century England; and as the "Levellers" and "Diggers" in the England of that age had shown, once one begins to take to pieces the social fabric and to question its origins, the process is difficult to stop.

Thus did the Age of Absolutism engender the instruments of its own destruction, or rather of its metamorphosis into the democratic absolutism of the Revolutionary and Napoleonic age. But it is well not to overlook the fact that the transition from belief to scepticism was neither a rapid nor an even process. It would manifestly be wrong to believe that the religious issues of preceding ages had vanished with the end of the "wars of religion"—with the Peace of Westphalia in 1648. On the contrary, the map of Europe according to religions—Orthodox, Catholic, Uniate and Protestant—must always be superimposed upon the maps of Europe according to racial stock, language and social pattern, to make intelligible the politics of our period, as indeed of much later ones. And where the religious frontier was not clear-cut, where Catholic overlapped with Protestant as in western Germany, or where Catholic, Uniate and Orthodox collided on the disputed and moving border between Russia and her western neighbours, new possibilities of conflict still existed. Nor where Christian Europe met the Moslem East in the Mediterranean or the Balkans had a still deeper and more ancient conflict ceased to have meaning. As late as 1716, Pope Clement XI was talking of a crusade against the Turk.

If on the international scene, such motives now played a secondary part as compared with the greed of dynasts or of expanding mercantile economies, if the Turk was not so much an infidel to be annihilated as a counter in the diplomatic game, as indeed he had been at least since the alliance between Francis I of France and the Sultan in the second quarter of the sixteenth century, the internal politics of European countries were still dominated by the belief—almost universal—in the desirability of religious conformity, for political reasons if for no others. It was in this age after all, that the French religious compromise enshrined in the Edict of Nantes broke down. In cancelling his grandfather's guarantee to his Protestant subjects in 1685 and in sharpening the persecution against them, Louis XIV not only exacerbated European suspicions of his intentions abroad but contributed, in the long run, to widening the gap between the French monarchy and important classes among his subjects. So too, the persecution that befell the Jansenist element within the Catholic fold was not without its political effects.

The religious issues were consequently now fought out for the most part within the framework of the several states, rather than internationally. The failure of Louis XIV to make good his efforts to sustain a Catholic Stuart dynasty on the English throne might be regarded as a postscript to the wars of religion properly speaking. In the second half of the eighteenth century, this change is marked by the almost total effacement of the Papacy as a factor in European politics, and by the expulsion of its militia, the Jesuit order, from successive States at the behest of their Catholic monarchs, a process culminating in the dissolution of the order by Clement XIV in 1773. The renewed emphasis upon religion after 1789 as a counterweight to the godlessness of the French Revolution marks not only a new phase in the history of religious sentiment, but in many countries, a new era in the perennial problem of Church and State.

This new phase is, of course, linked with an even wider reaction against many of the dominant cultural attitudes of the enlightenment—a reaction to which the name romantic is often loosely attached. From this point of view and from others as well, it can be argued that the period that begins roughly in 1660 ends not in 1815, but a generation earlier. It has, indeed, been traditional to take the American and French Revolutions as a major dividing line in European history. But the implications of this tradition have not always been appreciated. It was in fact based upon a conviction easier to hold fifty years ago than today, that the essential process of modern history has been a process in the direction of greater democracy, meaning by this the more widespread participation of the masses of the people in the regulation of their political affairs. From this point of view, the previous period, the period of the *ancien régime* was above all to be regarded as an age of class privilege in which the keys of power, both economic and political were firmly gripped by restricted social groups, landed or urban oligarchies, under whose selfish domination the many were ruthlessly exploited for the benefit of the few and whose cultural creations were to be seen as merely a veneer over the depths of primitive poverty and ignorance. The main historical interest of the era looked at in this light was in the accumulation of discontent, and in the development of new social forces and new systems of belief, under whose combined assault the older systems of power eventually crumbled. The American and French Revolutions were important not only for themselves, but in the example that they provided for others to follow. The fate of all empires was prefigured, it was thought, in the downfall of British dominion in America, and that of all monarchies in the collapse of the French Bourbons.

In our longer perspective such a view may seem superficial. Although the democratic principle has continued to make strides not only in the western world, but even in those parts of the globe that were in the eighteenth century only just beginning to fall under western influence, the principle itself has undergone many changes of interpretation, and has aroused violent and at times successful reactions. The ideas and programmes that the eighteenth-century revolutionaries believed to be indissolubly connected with the democratic principle have proved by no means so simply inter-related.

The famous triad of revolutionary France, "liberty, equality and fraternity", has failed to preserve its hypothetical unity. It is hard to see that liberty (as eighteenth-century thinkers would for the most part have defined it) has made important advances except in limited areas, and for limited periods of time. Equality after the French Revolution made gigantic strides in the social sense. It took only two generations to uproot from the Continent the predial serfdom that had for centuries provided the base of a relatively rigid class structure, enshrined in law as well as in custom. But economic inequality was actually fortified for a time by the impact of the new industrial order, before provoking the mighty egalitarian reaction of our own day. Finally, fraternity has found little or no scope among the conflicting nation-states, empires and races that have battled for hegemony or survival in the nineteenth and twentieth century worlds.

The movement towards a theory of economic individualism, in the second half of the eighteenth century, whether under the "legal despotism" postulated by the French physiocrats or in the more liberal guise given to it by the Adam Smith school was relatively short-lived. The basic social doctrine of the preceding era, the complex system of State intervention and control known as mercantilism, that seemed so totally discredited not only by the arguments of its critics but by events themselves, re-emerged in a new guise at the end of the nineteenth century and became the accepted canon in practice, if not in theory, for the most benevolent and respectable of governments.

Indeed from our own point of view, as has been suggested earlier, the century before the French Revolution is of special significance precisely because of the development of governmental techniques that were to be appropriated by the successors of the absolutist regimes that created them. Ever since Tocqueville's *Ancien Régime*—that is to say for almost a century— it has been a platitude of historical writing to point out that the French monarchy by its levelling and destroying tendencies paved the way for the achievements of Revolutionary and Napoleonic France, that the institutions of modern France, most of which appear to date from that era, represent only an adaptation of the earlier practices of monarchical absolutism. That absolutism was limited partly, as Tocqueville saw, by the existence of intermediary powers in the shape of privileged classes or centres of local autonomy, but also because of the fact that outside of those groups through whom power was actually exercised, its reliance had perforce to be upon a passive obedience that could not easily, or for long, be brought to undergo major sacrifices for public ends. These restraints disappeared when loyalty to the State was given a new warmth by its identification with a community. Rousseau's notion of the "general will" has been the butt of logicians ever since the *Social Contract* first appeared; but within a generation of his death the reality of the concept in practical politics was being dramatically and conclusively affirmed by the conduct of Revolutionary France, and in the struggle against France of other national groups. Democracy, it was found by 1815, could call forth energies that no absolute monarch had been able to utilize for long; and subsequent history has seen governments consistently exploit this fact. French conscription and the British income-tax, the two great weapons of the modern State were both creations of the 1790s. The "Age of Absolutism", as we have defined it, comes to an end only to give way to the new age of "Democratic Absolutism" that is our own.

With this in mind, it may be seen that to choose for consideration the period 1660–1815, and to call it the "Age of Absolutism", indicates an intention to concentrate upon the development of political and administrative institutions, upon the social forces that contributed to their development, and upon the presuppositions that underlay, consciously or not, their creation and employment. Since the period after 1789 involves so much besides, and since it is in its own right the most studied and most familiar of all periods of European history, it will be dealt with here largely by way of postscript, by way of an attempt to show the prolongation into it of the tendencies of the preceding age—an age not only further removed from us in time, but one whose atmosphere is much harder to enter into, and about which historians still have much to learn. And even here, we shall be forced to concentrate upon the years 1715–89 during which the institutions of monarchial absolutism reached the culminating point of their development

If we look back over the century and more of European history that end for the diplomat with the four peace treaties of the mid-seventeenth century—the Peace of Westphalia in 1648, the Peace of the Pyrenees in 1659 and the Treaties of Oliva and Copenhagen which ended the northern wars in 1660 —its striking feature is the complexity of the forces that were in armed conflict. The phrase, "The wars of religion" turns out to be only a name for a struggle whose participants included political organizations of all types and sizes from city-states to the multi-national empires of the Habsburgs or the Turkish Sultans, as well as national groups, social classes and religious organizations whose loyalty was to themselves in the first place, and often to themselves alone.

It becomes clear that despite the well-established habit of talking of the "new monarchies" of the late fifteenth and early sixteenth centuries, the political world of the next hundred and fifty years still showed the deep imprint of a feudalism that had nominally ceased to exist. The Middle Ages did not suddenly come to an end because an Italian sailor in Spanish service made landfall in the West Indies, or because a renegade German monk hurled defiance at Pope and Emperor.

The characteristic feature of feudalism, and of the Middle Ages, the intimate association of political power with the ownership of land showed considerable powers of survival. The petty autocracies of the Imperial knights of Germany lingered on as living reminders of the fact, just as the shadowy precedence accorded to the Imperial title lingered on after the power of its holders, the Austrian Habsburgs was reduced to that which they could exercise in their own hereditary lands.

In the sixteenth and seventeenth centuries, the modern idea of political sovereignty, the notion that over every man and every foot of ground, there must exist some single supreme authority was still something to be argued and fought over rather than the underlying presumption of all political action. Our ordinary technique of printing maps with a separate colour for each country can be very misleading indeed when applied to earlier ages, if one tries to draw from it conclusions about the relative strength of the units thus apparently comparable. The process by which maps of this kind came to be a faithful representation of the facts was still incomplete in 1660 in most of Europe, and in parts of Europe was scarcely complete until the drastic tidying-up of the Napoleonic era itself.

It was a process, however, that had been given an important impulse by the acceptance, as a foundation of the European religious settlement that general exhaustion had made essential, of a principle, first adumbrated in Germany a century earlier, that of *cujus regio, ejus religio*. This is usually interpreted as permitting each Prince to determine the religion of his subjects, and to compel uniformity by the sanction of expulsion. As such, we have noted its use by Louis XIV. On the other hand it was a principle that could work both ways. A would-be ruler might be forced to adopt his subjects' religion as Henry IV of France had done in 1593, as Frederick Augustus of Saxony was to do in 1697 in order to become King of Poland as Augustus II, and as the Stuart Pretenders to the throne of England were to refuse to do, to the credit of their consciences but the permanent blighting of their hopes. From the political point of view what mattered was that if it was for the State to decide how the individual should conduct his relations with the Deity, it was difficult in logic to deny it powers in matters less important. Thomas Hobbes was perfectly right in thinking that the main challenge to Leviathan sprang from the counter-claims of the Church.

Other claimants to political allegiance had also suffered during the wars; and the decline of urban-life along the old transcontinental trade-routes, particularly in Germany, had removed an important potential rival to the territorial Prince. The territorial Princes could now be recognized universally as competent to answer for the peaceful intentions of even their mightiest subjects; and the peace-settlements were based upon this conception of their position. It is therefore not hard to see why it is from these treaties of the mid-seventeenth century that the States-system of modern Europe essentially derives. Later wars were fought to modify these decisions; and later treaties embodied the modifications. Even the great upheaval of the Revolutionary and Napoleonic wars did not sweep away this structure though they refashioned and simplified it; and when the short lived creations of Napoleonic statesmanship in Germany and Italy passed away, the foundations of the old order remained for the Congress of Vienna to build upon.

But one must not forget that this consolidation of the position of the territorial sovereigns as against each other, did not imply in itself a full measure of authority in other respects. Nor, of course, can one describe it as though one were concerned with the modern impersonal nation-state. During the Thirty Years' War the sentiment of nationality had not been altogether absent; but the national group as such was not recognized in public law, and neither Czechs nor Catalans (to name two of the vanquished national groups) found independent representation in the final settlement. And even the State, apart from the monarch or dynasty, was still something of an abstraction over most of Europe.

Between 1660 and 1789, the important Powers forming part of the European states-system were all monarchies with the exception of Venice, and (to some degree) of the Netherlands, where the Stadtholders of the House of Orange retained their unique and anomalous position until the death of William III in

1702 and regained it in 1747. The system was therefore one which except in Poland presupposed as its foundation the hereditary rights of monarchs, and was thus still bound up with all the contingencies of individual life. In such circumstances, the political map of the western world was tributary to the accidents of the family relationship.

It is true that rules of succession within the different dynasties had been established for centuries in some cases; but except where there was a direct male heir, their prescriptions might differ even in the different dominions owing allegiance to a single sovereign. Since the fecundity of their subjects was rarely shared by the ruling houses, and since royal children were not immune from the high infant death rate of an unsanitary epoch, occasions for conflict were frequent and a constant temptation to the ambitious.

The failure of direct male heirs first to the Spanish, and then to the Austrian branch of the House of Habsburg, in 1700 and 1740, precipitated the two major European conflicts of the whole period before the Revolutionary wars. In the years after the death of Louis XIV, the whole course of French and European politics was affected by the rivalry between the French Regent, the Duke of Orleans, and Philip V of Spain, the two prospective claimants to the French throne should Louis XV not survive his sickly infancy, and by the efforts of the Emperor Charles VI to obtain through the adherence of the Powers to the Pragmatic Sanction a guarantee that the Austrian dominions might pass as a whole to his daughter.

Nor was dynasticism easily uprooted. In England which had led the world in the beheading of kings, the fiction of abdication was required to make the Revolution of 1688 respectable, and the non-juring schism in the Anglican Church showed how uneasy consciences could be about departing from the hereditary principle even when the lawful claimant was a Catholic. Until after 1745, the Jacobite danger was or seemed to be a political reality and the "age of Walpole" may easily be misunderstood if this is not appreciated. From 1714 until 1837, a common Crown linked the fortunes of Britain and Hanover. On the Continent the principle was even stronger. Napoleon's Habsburg marriage was testimony to his appreciation of its vitality; and dynasticism

was the core of the notion of legitimacy with which the states-
men at the Vienna Congress sought to repair the ravages of the
great usurper.

The essentially competitive nature of the dynastic system
drove the monarchs along the road which was to lead to their
ultimate destruction. Their objective internally was bound to
be that of creating an ever greater measure of efficiency. The
fate of Poland—still a Great Power in 1660—was a reminder of
what might happen should the social or political foundations for
such efficiency prove absent. But to create efficiency meant
to organize and institutionalize their loyal power to build up
an impersonal bureaucracy, to complete the process by which
the Court shed responsibility for the practical as distinct
from the ceremonial functions of kingship, to develop a
financial system by which the revenues necessary for public
purposes should no longer be inseparable from the private
income of the king, considered simply as a landowner—in other
words to assist in the birth of the modern State. And the modern
State has no need of the hereditary absolute monarch.

Such a consummation was foreseen, if only dimly, long
before the Revolution itself. In France, after the death of
Louis XIV, the king and the court—Versailles and all it
stood for—seemed ever more separate from the productive and
active centre of French affairs at Paris. As d'Argenson—
administrator and statesman as well as *philosophe*—wrote
"absolute monarchical government is excellent under a good
king; but who will guarantee that we shall always have a Henry
IV?" Montesquieu—the greatest thinker on political matters
of the first half of the eighteenth century—denounced in
classic passages the weaknesses and vices of courtiers. From
his time, although direct attacks on the person of the monarch
are still debarred, it is clear that the notion of the State is
replacing that of the Crown. "Today," wrote a French diarist of
the period—the Abbé de Véri—in 1779, "hardly anyone would
dare to say in Parisian circles: 'I serve the King'. That would be
left to the high flunkeys of Versailles. 'I serve the State': 'I have
served the State'; that is the common expression." And not
only "State" but with it "Nation" pass into common usage at
this time.

The idea of "Nation" is older than the idea of "State". But when the affairs of the nation were being carried on to its satisfaction by the monarch, there was no occasion, it seemed, to appeal to it directly. National sentiment, of which there are plenty of literary expressions in the sixteenth century for instance, was politically, a reserve force to be called on only in time of need. Such a moment seemed to some Frenchmen to have come in the later years of Louis XIV, when the European coalition that his ambitions had called into being against him, seemed to menace the French homeland itself. In August 1710, Fénelon, the former tutor of the Duke of Burgundy, heir to the throne, and the brain of the aristocratic opposition, wrote to the Duc de Chevreuse one of its leaders:

"Our misfortune arises from the fact that the war has hitherto been the affair of the king alone who is ruined and discredited. It must be made the real affair of the whole body of the nation. . . . It is necessary that there should be spread throughout our nation an intimate conviction that it is the nation itself that in its own interest bears the burden of this war. . . . It is for her to find the resources and to raise money wherever it can be found."

In such a passage as that, is foreshadowed the dynamic appeal of nationalism in the wars of Revolutionary France.

But to take the development of the State and the changes in political sentiment, as well as in political structure, which this involved to be the main theme of our study demands from the beginning a word of warning. Neither in this respect nor in any other can we speak of eighteenth-century Europe as a single unit. In western and central Europe, the aristocratic classes and the cultures they patronized stood for a certain internationalism; and the circulation of ideas in restricted circles especially the latter half of the century reached as far as St. Petersburg. But the development of institutions and of sentiments, though not unaffected in one country by what was happening in another, was bound to vary profoundly according to the different economies, social structures, legal traditions and national outlooks of the several peoples. The idea of a single process varying only slightly in speed from one country to another is as much of an illusion in the period which we are considering as it has proved in the nineteenth and twentieth centuries. Indeed the later history of the Continent can hardly be understood unless these historic singularities are appreciated at their full value. Talk of European union that was intermittent in the eighteenth century from the Abbé de St. Pierre at its beginning to Immanuel Kant at its end had little meaning, because of the toughness of this substantial bedrock of diversity.

Reference has been made to the importance of the manifold religious divisions of Europe. Equally significant in the long run was the difference in economic and social experience as between one part and another, equally significant, but much less known. It is only very recently that the statistical information to whose manifest imperfections reference has already been made, has been brought together for the purposes of economic historians. Only within the last few years have the new techniques of economic analysis been applied to the questions of wages and prices in the pre-industrial era. And the geographical distribution of such investigations in still a very uneven one.

The general nature of the regional divisions of the Continent is, however, fairly clear. The decay of the German cities other than Hamburg is not the only example of the fact that economic decline—a relative as well as an absolute notion—is as significant as economic advance. Indeed for an Englishman or a Dutchman, the difficulty is to realize how exceptional was the nature of their countries' commercial ascent in the latter half of the sixteenth, and earlier half of the seventeenth centuries, and the consequent advance in their social and political life of a commercial bourgeoisie. So far from the position of the bourgeoisie improving in the remainder of Mediterranean and Western Europe, it would be correct save perhaps in France, to talk of a strengthening of the landed nobility at its expense. The great days of the Italian city-state as well as of the Hanseatic and other German cities were over—how far is fifteenth-century Florence recognizable in the Grand Duchy of Tuscany or the Medici banker in his Grand-Ducal descendant? Even in France which shared in part in the profits of this earlier commercial and industrial revolution, a city like Lyons had seen better days.

Although Bordeaux and Nantes grew on the profits of sugar and slaves, and Marseilles on the Levant trade, as one left the coasts of the English Channel and the North Sea one passed outside the radius of mercantile supremacy.

Still sharper was the division between western and central Europe as a whole and eastern Europe, where commercial life had always been restricted and where indigenous middle-classes had hardly developed. In Europe west of the Elbe the economic trends of the age worked in favour of the growth of a cash nexus between landlord and tenant, between owner of the soil and tiller, and against the continued exaction of personal labour services. England was an exception in the early and total collapse of villeinage; elsewhere right up to the Revolution, the issue was undecided, and progress uneven. But, by and large, the disappearance of labour services and with them of the legally inferior status that they carried was the dominant process. Personal freedom was becoming the normal thing. To revive an unfashionable nineteenth-century terminology, the movement of western European society in the latter half of the seventeenth century and in the first half of the succeeding one was a movement from "status" to "contract", or if one prefers it, from castes to classes.

But in eastern Europe—for a variety of reasons, some economic as in the granary of the Vistula basin, some political as in Russia—the tendency was precisely the contrary one. The cultivator was attached ever more rigorously to the soil; peasantry became almost synonymous with serfdom, social and political power was the monopoly of those who could command the services of this depressed majority. So far, from a ladder of advancement tempering the inequalities between the classes, the structure became more, not less, rigid. Indeed to the barriers of caste might be added barriers of nationality. As in conquered Bohemia or expanding Hungary, or still swollen Poland and Turkey the speech and even the religion of the dominant minority might differ from that of the toiling mass. And even a third division might be added where yet another foreign element—Jews in Poland, Germans in the cities of Danubian Europe—came in to perform those middle-class functions, for which the aristocracies were too proud, and the rural masses too illiterate and too depressed. Unless this dramatic contrast between East and West is appreciated, there is no beginning of understanding either this period or its successors.

In conclusion, it must be admitted that in talking of Europe in the Age of Absolutism by itself one is doing violence to historical reality. By 1660 the conflicts of the European sovereigns had long had repercussions outside the geographical limits of the Continent. The speed of discovery since the great maritime advance of fifteenth-century Portugal had been uneven, and the exploitation of such discoveries even more so. Central and Southern America, the eastern seaboard of North America and what is now Indonesia had all felt a major impact from European expansionism. The great conflict for the North American interior was only just beginning. India itself and the slave coasts of Africa were affected to a lesser extent. But little difference had been made to the world as yet, by the Russian "conquest" of Siberia, or the arrival of Muscovites on the shores of the Pacific.

Nevertheless, the importance of these territories, and of the contest for their political control that was to form the backcloth to European history properly speaking, were not fully realized in this period. Major resources were still reserved for use nearer home. Private adventure curbed by the State at home still had elbow-room in other continents. For the crusading baron of the Middle Ages or the condottiere of the Renaissance, one must look in the eighteenth century to Englishmen and Frenchmen in India. Only slowly did some of the States of Europe catch up with their new opportunities and new responsibilities. The dwarfing of Europe, particularly of western Europe, that is the major historical phenomenon of our own generation, could hardly be foreseen when it seemed that the rest of the world was Europe's for the taking. From our present viewpoint, much eighteenth-century history is a bit parochial.

CHAPTER II

THE EUROPEAN SCENE: 1660–1789

Of all forms of history, diplomatic history is the least profitable. Volumes have been filled with the complicated series of negotiations punctuated at intervals by wars, and of wars only temporarily interrupted by treaties, that go to make up the outward story of international or rather inter-state relations in the last century and a half of the *ancien régime*. Our concern with these transactions lies in two directions: the changes in the map of Europe and its overseas possessions brought about by war, and registered by treaty, and the effect of war and its burdens upon the internal structure of the states concerned.

The period between 1660 and 1789 affords one of the classic instances of a states-system, based upon an accepted condition of permanent rivalry between independent political units; and as has already been seen, contemporary reflections of a more or less utopian nature upon the desirability and prospects of perpetual peace bore little relation to contemporary realities. War was throughout, regarded as the normal method of settling disputes. Its largely professional character and the consequent limitation upon the proportion of national resources devoted to it, as well as the lack of ideological fervour among the combatants, prevented the emergence of the haunting fears of earlier and of more recent times, that the outcome might be the total destruction of civilization. War did not prevent the rapid growth of population that set in, as has been seen about the middle of the eighteenth century, nor some measure of economic advance. There was nothing to parallel the great devastation of the Thirty Years War.

The endemic character of warfare in this age was partly, perhaps, a result of this relative lack of destructiveness, and of the fact that contemporary developments in weapons, and in strategic theory, made armies slow-moving and costly caravans not lightly risked far from their bases of supply, and rarely hazarded in decisive engagements. Only in the last decades of the *ancien régime* did developments in weapons and in military doctrine pave the way for the Napoleonic transformation of warfare by armies whose cadres (like Napoleon himself) owed their training to its schools. But this relative innocuousness, though it may explain why less time was needed to recover from war, does not itself explain its causes. One contributing factor was, no doubt, the subordination of economic life generally speaking to the requirements of States—even a critic of mercantilism like Adam Smith gave defence priority over "affluence". Economic policies were calculated on a beggar-my-neighbour basis, the possession of territory at home or overseas being regarded as giving exclusive rights to the exploitation of its economic resources. Monopoly and protectionism were at once the causes and the weapons of conflict. In the second place, there was a development of the social phenomenon known as militarism. By this is meant the connexion of war, and of preparation for war, with the interest and prestige of particular social groups, excluded by choice or necessity from other occupations. And this was true in different degrees of the landed aristocracy over most of Europe. Indeed the experience of previous generations might well suggest that the most likely result of a cessation of outlets for external warfare, would simply be to ignite the flames of civil strife.

Like the Italy of the fifteenth century, Europe in the "Age of Absolutism" fought its wars with the aid of professional armies. But these were now more firmly interlocked with the machinery of the State which was, indeed, very largely occupied with problems of their recruitment, training and maintenance. The standing army on land was a comparatively new thing, and even when still partially recruited from foreign sources, like Britain's "Hessians" in the War of American Independence, it was thoroughly subordinated to the purpose of the rulers. A military career could not now bring independent political power irrespective of birth. There were no more international captains to sell their swords and their power of raising men to the highest bidder, though the sale of recruits was not unknown as a method of raising revenues by the lesser German Princes and the Swiss. The career of a Wallenstein could no longer make kings and emperors tremble; although the Balkan exploits of the Habsburgs' best general Prince Eugene of Savoy were sometimes ascribed by contemporaries to personal ambition, and in India, a Clive could still carve out a fortune with his sword.

At sea, the picture was rather different, with the privateer still continuing to play an important rôle in war time. The heavy expenses involved in keeping up a standing navy on the British model were not always regarded as worth while, even by so wealthy a country as France, which after the naval defeat of La Hogue in 1692, tended more often than not to rely on the prowess of its privateering commerce destroyers.

For the next century sea-power except in the Mediterranean made itself felt in the struggle for overseas empire, rather than in Europe. Its results can be chronicled briefly.

During this earlier period, when sugar from the West Indies was still the most important rival to the spices of the Orient among Europe's imports from overseas, the British maintained their important foothold in the Caribbean Sea; the French (and to a lesser extent the Dutch and the Danes) did likewise. The result was that Spain and Portugal lost their chance to keep as their own preserve, their mainland Empires in Central and South America. In North America, the British thrust from the cis-Appalachian coastline finally broke through the attempted French encirclement linking the mouths of the St. Lawrence and the Mississippi. By 1763, the whole Continent seemed to lie open to British expansion, except for the rather inchoate northward prongs of Spanish penetration from Mexico.

In Asia the device of the chartered company somewhat muffled the reverberations of the conflict, where the home governments were concerned. But in the last resort, perhaps, Clive's triumph over Dupleix was due to a greater appreciation in Britain than in France, of the significance of the Indian theatre. And with the defeat of Dupleix, France's opportunities of Indian Empire received a final setback. In Indonesia and Ceylon the Dutch were still ensconced in the positions won from the Portuguese pioneers. In Africa alone, no decision was reached in this period. All the maritime and colonizing nations still traded along its coasts for the products of the interior, in particular for the human cargoes upon which the valorization of much of their American dominions depended. The Dutch retained their position at the Cape of Good Hope as a station on the route to the Indies.

But the later importance of these decisions was still not realized and it was (outside Britain at any rate) the changes in the political control of European countries with their denser populations, their compact civilizations and developed economies that were regarded not unnaturally by contemporaries as the most important consequences of the struggles between dynasties and States. Nor were such changes unimportant for the people whose allegiance was affected by the redistribution of debated lands, or by the accession of new dynasties with new interests and affiliations, or for later generations. For these peoples when they came later on to embrace the doctrine of national self-determination, found that they had inherited a political map of Europe much of which might seem to have been drawn with the express purpose of frustrating their ambitions.

Bearing in mind what has been said about the limitations of political geography in an age before the consolidation of State power, and about the inadequacy of population statistics, it is nevertheless desirable to give some reminder of the geographical layout of Europe at the opening of our period in 1660.

The Bourbon monarch of France, Louis XIV, who had just attained his majority, found that his compact and fertile territories gave him the greatest accumulation of power in the hands of any single monarch. His subjects at home numbered perhaps nineteen or twenty millions—a level at which the population of France had according to some opinions been relatively stationary for three centuries, but which was actually, it appears, to decline to about 18,000,000 in 1710, as a result of war, famine and disease. Even so, the numerical predominance in Europe of the French people is as important for the understanding of the Age of Absolutism as their cultural leadership which was certainly not wholly unconnected with it.

The Spanish branch of the House of Habsburg, France's principal rival in the wars just ended, ruled over a land whose population was generally thought to be in decline, and which may perhaps have numbered only about 5,000,000, compared with the 8,000,000 of its sixteenth-century golden age. In addition to Spain proper, other important territories owed allegiance to Philip IV. These were: on France's north eastern frontier, the Spanish Netherlands, covering a rather larger area than the modern Belgium and Luxemburg, and further south another portion of the old Burgundian inheritance, the Franche-Comté; in Italy, the Milanese, the Kingdom of Naples and Sicily, and the island of Sardinia; and in America, the vast empire, source of Spain's wealth, and as some would argue, of its political and economic decline by the sapping of its productive energies, and the unbalancing of its economy through the effect of its excessive imports of specie.

When Philip IV died in 1665 to be succeeded by the four-year-old Charles II, the prolongation of whose sickly existence to 1700 upset all reasonable expectation, there began the long struggle, military and diplomatic, for the succession. The Franco-Spanish "War of Devolution" in the 1660s, the Franco-Dutch war in the 1670s, the War of the League of Augsburg which lasted for a decade from 1688, and finally after Charles's death, the War of the Spanish Succession, properly so-called—all these are related to the central determination of the French to prevent anything like a revival of the unitary Habsburg dominion of the sixteenth-century Emperor Charles V, and to secure new acquisitions on all their borders. The peace-treaties of Louis XIV's reign: Aix-la-Chapelle (1668) Nimwegen (1678), Ryswick (1697), Utrecht (1713), and Rastatt (1714) mark successive stages in the achievement of some of these objectives.

The French war (1672–8) against the United Provinces (the modern Holland) comes into this picture, as does the Dutch participation in the later wars under William III, and through Heinsius' collaboration with Marlborough. This is because soon after the Dutch had achieved their independence of Spain, it began to be clear that it was the French rather than the Spaniards who now presented a danger to them, despite the traditional link between the Republican (or anti-Orange party) and a pro-French foreign policy. The maintenance of Habsburg sovereignty in the Southern Netherlands (the modern Belgium) as a barrier against French encroachment was thus a major

Dutch interest. And when in 1714 the country finally passed from Spanish to Austrian rule, a literal barrier in the form of fortresses paid for by the Belgians, but garrisoned by the Dutch, remained a feature of the European strategic and political scene.

The exhaustion caused by the long European wars following upon the earlier maritime conflict with England, and the burden of trying to maintain their position were to help cause the Dutch to sink in the course of the eighteenth century, to a secondary status among the Powers. But in 1660, this small country of 2,000,000 was, thanks to its commerce and its banks, its navy and its dykes, an unmistakable Great Power capable of standing up to England in one decade and to France in the next. It was to Holland that moralizing economists turned for lessons in what we now call productivity; and it is to the Holland of that period as mirrored in its arts, that we look for the model of the urban bourgeois civilization of the age—a sober contrast to the brilliant flamboyance of the French court. It was this people whose protestantism, republicanism and commercial success made them particularly odious to Louis XIV, as the representative of catholicism, divine right monarchy and martial chivalry with all its wanton extravagance.

England, the other maritime Protestant power had (including Wales) a population at this period of over 5,000,000 and reconquered Ireland about 1,000,000 more—a population whose religious and national animosity to the conquerors made it scarcely a political asset. Scotland, though owing allegiance to the same royal house was politically and economically a separate unit, as it remained until 1707. Its 1,000,000 or so inhabitants did not, until after that date, share in the rising prosperity of their southern neighbours; and not until after the suppression of the "Forty-Five" were the Highlands brought fully within the orbit of the central government, and the anachronism of their social structure swept away.

The other principal power involved in the struggle for overseas empire was Portugal which in 1665, finally repulsed Spanish attempts to prolong a dominion over it that had lasted unbroken from 1580 to 1640. From this period dates Portugal's close association with Great Britain for whom it provided in the War of the Spanish Succession, as again a hundred years later in the

Napoleonic era, a possible backdoor for entry into western Europe. The eighteenth-century English Whig could pledge the downfall of the Bourbon monarchies in bumpers of port, while the taste for claret once the mark of England's long abandoned rule over Gascony, remained to cheer the Tory advocates of peace with France. But Portugal itself with its 2,000,000 inhabitants no longer possessed the élan that had made its history in the fifteenth and sixteenth centuries so full of enterprise and adventure; it was in 1660 despite the growing wealth of Brazil a Power quite clearly of secondary rank.

The only country which could have competed with France by virtue of its population was Germany, the number of whose inhabitants in 1660 perhaps exceeded the 20,000,000 mark, despite the losses of the Thirty Years War. But after the Peace of Westphalia, Germany with its 300 virtually independent sovereignties of all sizes, was more than ever a geographical expression without seemingly, any marked sense of common nationality to counterbalance its political incoherence. The nominal pre-eminence of the Holy Roman Emperor was more shadowy than ever, now that the Peace of Westphalia had given both France and Sweden a say in the Imperial Diet, in virtue of their German conquests. For positive co-operation from the Princes, the Emperor's only serious recourse was individual bargains; it did not promise much.

The Emperor himself—and the election of the heir to the Austrian Habsburgs was a foregone conclusion so long as the male line endured—owed his own position to the lands that he held by hereditary right: Austria proper, Bohemia, Silesia and such part of Hungary as was not under the Turk—in 1660 a comparatively narrow strip. In all, at that date, he ruled over perhaps 6,000,000 or 7,000,000 people. When the Emperor Charles VI died in 1740, leaving only a daughter Maria Theresa, Charles the Elector of Bavaria, with the support of France and Spain conquered Bohemia and secured election as King by the Bohemian Estates, in defiance of their pledges to Maria Theresa, and in 1742, election as the Emperor Charles VII. But without the Habsburg lands, the title itself was meaningless. After Charles's death in 1745, the Imperial title was conferred upon Francis of Lorraine, Maria Theresa's husband; and it

passed from him to their son Joseph II. The ambition of
Charles VI to leave the Habsburg lands undivided to his
daughter which had inspired his seeking the assent of the
European powers to the "Pragmatic Sanction", by which he had
tried to forestall an appeal to the ancient so-called "Salic Law"
against female succession, had thus been fulfilled except for
Prussia's conquest of Silesia. But the outcome was a Habsburg
not an imperial triumph. When therefore in 1806, Francis II
(Joseph II's nephew) declared the Holy Roman Empire at
an end after 1,006 years of continuous history, and continued
to reign as Francis I, hereditary Emperor of Austria, the title he
had adopted two years previously, he was merely accepting a
fact which the Napoleonic reshaping of Germany had made
obvious, namely that the Imperial title had long been a meaningless and embarrassing shadow.

Of the Emperor's nominal vassals in 1660, four were
considerable territorial sovereigns. The Elector of Brandenburg
ruled over perhaps 2,000,000 people in his scattered dominions
which included, besides the nuclear domain of Brandenburg
and its adjacent lands, important territories in the west of
Germany, and in the east, the Duchy of East Prussia, over
which Poland had but recently renounced her suzerainty, and
which was separated from the rest of Germany by a broad belt
of Polish land. Saxony, Bavaria and Hanover each had at this
time between one and two million inhabitants. Each of them
was to have a separate and contrasting fate in the eighteenth
century: Saxony through its dynastic connexion with Poland,
after the choice of its Elector as King of Poland in 1697;
Hanover through its dynastic link with England from 1714, and
Bavaria as the most consistent standby of French diplomacy in
its endeavours to frustrate the plans of the Habsburgs.

Brandenburg whose ruler was crowned King of Prussia in
1701 was the only one of these German states to achieve the
status of a Great Power. French patronage was partly responsible for its early successes; but in 1756, the famous reversal of
alliances linked France with its old enemy, Austria, against the
rising menace of a Prussia now allied to Britain.

Poland whose decline was inherent in Prussia's rise still
contained in 1660 vast territories stretching from the mouth of

the Vistula and the coastline of the vassal Duchy of Courland, to within striking distance of the Black Sea outlets of the Dnieper and Dniester, where it faced the Tartar vassals of the Turks. The population of Poland probably numbered over 6,000,000, and has been reckoned at over 11,000,000 on the eve of the partitions. But it was neither racially homogeneous nor politically stable. Polish expansion eastwards in the late sixteenth and early seventeenth century as the eastern arm of the Counter-Reformation had extended its rule over Orthodox peoples. Conversion had been largely confined to the land-owning classes except for the compromise enshrined in the Uniate Church in its southern territories, where allegiance to the Pope had been achieved at the price of considerable concessions to local custom in liturgy and discipline. A reviving Russian State would not have far to look for pretexts for intervention; and the fight on the eastern marches between Catholic and Orthodox was to be renewed in the eighteenth century with the chances in Russia's favour.

The constitutional difficulties of the Polish State were inseparable from the economic dominance of the landowners, who had managed to preserve both an elective kingship, and a Diet in which any attempts at serious centralization could be checked. This double handicap was too much for any Polish king to hope to overcome.

Poland and Brandenburg-Prussia, and by the end of the seventeenth century, Russia as well, were all rivals of the Scandinavian Powers in the tangled politics of the Baltic area, upon whose southern coasts a predominantly Germanic aristocracy ruled a medley of peasant peoples of Slav and Finno-Ugrian stock. With the decline of the German Hansa, local predominance seemed destined to pass to the territorial powers of the Baltic littoral; but there were also the interests to be considered of the two North Sea maritime powers, England and Holland, for whom the products of the Baltic mines and forests were the main source of the materials out of which their vessels were constructed. Only when the later eighteenth century saw a growth in the supplies of these things that Britain in particular, could obtain from across the Atlantic, did Baltic politics become of less acute importance to the West.

And not till after our period was over, did technical developments reduce the Baltic to its modern status of an inland sea.

Even in the seventeenth century the possibilities of dominating the entry to the Baltic and of exacting dues—the "Sound dues"—from its users, were what gave its importance to the poor and thinly populated kingdom of Denmark (which included Norway). Sweden with its 1,500,000 inhabitants had probably a rather larger population than Denmark; and it had emerged from the Thirty Years War and from the northern wars of the mid-century, with considerable accessions of territory. In 1660, the Swedes ruled Finland, the whole southern coast of the Baltic east of the mouth of the Dvina, as well as Western Pomerania and its off-shore islands, which gave control of the River Oder. By holding on to another strip of land between the mouths of the rivers Elbe and Weser, Sweden also retained a window on the North Sea.

In the East, the vast territories of Russia were still cut off from both the Baltic and the Black Sea, and faced to the south and south-east a long-debated frontier land where Cossack colonies and Tartar tribes were both dependent on their own skilled savagery rather than on the far off rulers at Moscow and Constantinople. Russia's population may have been about 8,000,000 perhaps in 1680, by which time the Ukraine east of the Dnieper and most of White Russia had passed from Polish to Russian rule by the truce of Andrusovo.

Even less statistical information is forthcoming about she Ottoman Empire. Turkish rule in 1660 lay thinly but oppressively over the whole of the Balkan peninsula and the Hungarian plain, and eastwards to the Dniester, over the Crimea and the shores of the sea of Azov, as well as over the whole of the eastern and nearly the whole of the southern shores of the Mediterranean.

Of the historic names of the European peoples, one does not appear on the map at all. Italy even more than Germany was a geographical expression. The 11,000,000 or so Italians (a figure which rose to 15,000,000 by 1789) had no political instrument at all through which to express a sense of nationality no less developed than that of their neighbours. The dominant power in Italian affairs in 1660 was Spain which, as has been seen, ruled directly over much of the country. Of the other territorial powers, five were of more than local significance: the Papal states—more for the unique character of their rulers than for their own extent or resources, Tuscany, Genoa with her Ligurian littoral, Savoy, already engaged in he perilous but profitable game of balancing its control of the Alpine passes against concessions from the major Powers, and finally Venice, still struggling to retain the scattered outpost of its former Adriatic, Ionian and Aegean empires.

It has already been pointed out that the half century after 1660 was dominated by the ambitions of Louis XIV. The wars which these ambitions set in motion became entangled with those that owed their origins to the conflict of the two principal contenders for Baltic supremacy, ultimately Charles XII of Sweden and Peter the Great (Peter I) of Russia, and with the long drawn out conflict on the frontiers of Turkey. For this reason the next suitable point for surveying the map of Europe is the year 1721 when a temporary halt to the fighting had been called by the treaties of Utrecht (1713), Rastatt (1714), Passarowitz (1718), Stockholm (1720) and Nystadt (1721).

France had something to show in the shape of gains from Spain: Franche Comtè and part of the southern Netherlands and in addition much of the Imperial territory of Alsace was by now also French, including the important city of Strasbourg. Spain now under a cadet branch of the House of Bourbon had lost the remainder of the southern Netherlands to the Austrian Habsburgs who retained them, as has been seen, in something less than full sovereignty, owing to the barrier fortresses accorded to the Dutch, and the servitude of the closing of the Scheldt imposed upon the Belgians so that Antwerp should not compete commercially with the ports of Holland. Spain had also been evicted from the Italian mainland, and had been replaced by Austria whose domination in the north was to endure (apart from the Napoleonic interlude) until the Risorgimento and the creation of united Italy. After a complicated series of transactions, the island of Sardinia passed to the Dukes of Savoy in 1720 bearing with it a royal title; and acquisitions in Piedmont by the same grasping dynasty faintly foreshadowed their later dominant rôle in the peninsula itself. Finally to England, Spain had lost both Gibraltar and Minorca (the latter to be recovered ultimately in 1783), and had thus provided British sea-power with its first permanent bases in Mediterranean waters.

In dynastic terms it might seem that the House of Bourbon was the great gainer from these changes, despite the victories of Marlborough and the gloom that overshadowed the last years of Louis XIV. But since Philip V had been forced to renounce his claim to the French throne at the price of his Spanish one, and since the French Regent was determined to see the renunciation upheld, relations between the two branches of the family were far from cordial at first. And although the Regent's death in 1723 removed this element of difficulty, it was not until the Family Compact of 1761 that the two branches of the family linked their fortunes and those of their countries in a manner that survived up to the Revolution.

From the territorial point of view, the profit by 1721 had gone to the Austrian Habsburgs. For, in addition to the gains in the Netherlands and in Italy, there had been mighty strides in the East. The whole of Hungary and Transylvania, most of Croatia, Slovenia, and Serbia, and part of Wallachia had passed from Ottoman to Habsburg rule. In 1684, the ancient Republic of Ragusa on the Adriatic accepted Habsburg suzerainty. But there was to be a great ebb from the high tide of Passarowitz before the advance was resumed. Venice, too, had made a striking advance at Turkish expense—in Dalmatia. But this was offset by the Turkish conquest of Crete.

Against the Russians, the Turks had been more fortunate, since the Russians found it difficult to consolidate their military gains and failed to establish themselves in Peter's reign upon the sea of Azov. Footholds gained from Persia by Peter on the Caspian were also to prove only temporary though they served to prevent a Turkish conquest there. Elsewhere the Russians had made important advances. The westward thrust against Poland had begun with the acquisitions of 1667; and if in 1721, there seemed no immediate pressure for further Russian expansion in this direction, it was largely because Poland under her weak Saxon kings was almost a vassal state herself. The collapse of Swedish power on the European mainland, of which there remained only a vestige in Pomerania, had also

redounded primarily to Russia's benefit, and given point to
the location on the River Neva, of Peter's new capital. The
other possible beneficiaries of Sweden's decline were Prussia
and Hanover—the former's steady devotion to the extension of
its territories having as yet brought no spectacular results.

These changes in political geography must not be taken too
literally as pointers to changes in relative power. Habsburg
power was actually weaker than it had been, partly owing to
Charles VI's increasing pre-occupation with the diplomacy of the
"Pragmatic Sanction". In the eighteenth century, the dynasty
was to become less and less concerned with western Europe to
which it was linked only by the outlying Belgium, and more and
more pre-occupied with its newly acquired non-German and
often non-Catholic subjects in south-eastern Europe. The
reversal of rôles as between Poland and Sweden on the one hand,
and Russia and Prussia on the other was also much more
pronounced than the territorial changes would indicate. The
Dutch apparently among the victor powers were entering upon
a period of decline, while Spain found the change of dynasty to
be the political equivalent of a blood-transfusion. Indeed the
ambitions of Philip V, or rather of his Italian wife Elizabeth
Farnese, were among the most disturbing elements in European
politics for the next two decades.

The 1720s were a period of alarums and excursions rather
than of large-scale warfare. But by the following decade, the
eighteenth century took on its characteristic pattern of endemic
warfare with the European rivalries of France, Spain, Austria,
Russia and Prussia inseparably entangled with the Anglo-
French and Anglo-Spanish struggle overseas. The latter was
still relatively quiescent during the first of the European wars—
the rather inadequately styled "War of the Polish Succession"
from 1733 to 1738. But with the "War of the Austrian Succession," 1740–8, the "Seven Years War" 1756–63, and finally,
"the War of American Independence" 1776–83, the two
struggles practically merged into one.

The history-book names of these wars conceal, in fact, a great
deal of complicated military and diplomatic history, since few
of the participants in any of them, remained at war throughout
the periods thus designated. In the last of these, too, the

non-maritime Powers were scarcely concerned. But the essential rivalries are not difficult to grasp. Until the "reversal of alliances" in 1756, the pattern was largely that of the preceding age—British support of the "old alliance" (that of 1689), with the Habsburgs against an aggressive France and Prussia. For a time Prussia was Britain's main continental ally, along with whatever other lesser supporters a policy of subsidy might bring. Russia as it came further into European politics tended at first to be pro-Habsburg and anti-Hohenzollern. But after 1763, the new issue of Polish partition dominated her relations with the Germanic powers. Thus the Anglo-French rivalry was (after the pacific era of Walpole and Fleury had come to an end in the early 1740s) the most enduring of all. Hence some historians write of all these events, and even of those up to 1815—as "the Second Hundred Years War".

The outcome in Europe by 1789 can again be traced in outline fashion upon the map. France continued to expand eastwards, adding to her possessions in Alsace, and finally in 1766, acquiring Lorraine which had been under predominantly French influence for a long time previously. Its last period of independence had been lived out under the rule of Stanislas Leszczinski, father-in-law to Louis XV, and France's successful candidate for the Polish throne in the 1730s. The elegant baroque of Nancy's "Place Stanislas" remains to remind one of this episode in the history of a much fought-over province. Meanwhile, the head of the house of Lorraine, Francis, had been compensated with the Dukedom of Tuscany which came to him upon the death of the last Medici in 1737, as well as with the hand of Maria Theresa, and ultimately, as has been seen, the imperial title.

In 1768, France also acquired, this time from Genoa, Venice's great maritime rival in the Middle Ages, the island of Corsica of which Rousseau had just written that it would one day astonish the world, as indeed it did, if not in the way that Rousseau imagined. For the French annexation was only just in time to make a Frenchman by birth of the Italian-descended Napoleon Bonaparte who was born at Ajaccio in 1769.

With a population that had passed the 25,000,000 mark,

France in 1789 was still the greatest power in Europe, though well surpassed by Russia as far as mere numbers were concerned. The population of England and Wales was now about 9,000,000, of Great Britain as a whole perhaps 15,000,000.

Austria had continued to lose ground in the west. To make up for the loss of Silesia to Prussia, there were only the gains made at Bavaria's expense in 1779. The more ambitious plan of exchanging Belgium for Bavaria itself had come to nothing, like so many of the great designs hatched at Vienna.

In the Balkans, Serbia, Bosnia and Wallachia had all passed back under Turkish rule in the disastrous Peace of Belgrade (1739). The acquisition of Bukovina in 1777 hardly compensated the Austrians for these losses. On the other hand this province had the merit of linking with Transylvania the large and important territories acquired from Poland in 1770 and 1772.

Perhaps 27,000,000 people in all were now ruled from Vienna. But the full implications of the changes can hardly be appreciated unless the polyglot character of the populations concerned is taken into account. The Czechs and Slovaks doubled their numbers in the eighteenth century—from 1,500,000 to 3,000,000. The Transylvanian population augmented by immigrants tripled from its 500,000 at the century's beginning; while Hungary's population grew from 1,500,000 to over 6,500,000. The latter, however, was due to the recolonization of the Hungarian plain after the final repulse of the Turks. The new colonists were by no means all of Magyar stock. Indeed when Austria finally had a census in 1804, of the 6,800,000 inhabitants of Hungary only 3,500,000 were Magyars; Roumanians, Croats, Serbs, Slovaks and Germans made up the rest. The Slavs increased most rapidly; but this did not hinder the consolidation of the Magyar aristocracy with its important consequences for the Austro-Hungary of the future.

Meanwhile, Prussia's growth had been continuous: Silesia was annexed in 1740, East Friesland in 1744, West Prussia and other Polish territories in 1772 (the ancient free city of Danzig retaining a precarious independence till 1793), and Mansfeld in central Germany in 1780. Frederick William II, who had succeeded his uncle Frederick II in 1786, ruled between

8,000,000 and 9,000,000 people; but except for the Poles, acquired in 1772, and immigrants such as the French Huguenots attracted by Frederick II's calculated generosity, his subjects were all German, and in as far as German national feeling was, or was to become a factor, Prussia could fairly claim to rival Austria as its political expression.

In Italy, after many complicated transactions, Elizabeth Farnese's hopes for her descendants had been amply fulfilled, since Bourbon dynasties ruled in the Kingdom of the Two Sicilies and in Parma, balancing junior branches of the Habsburgs in Modena and Tuscany. The Italians whom a century of relative peace and some prosperity had multiplied to a total of perhaps 18,000,000, might seem as far from unity as ever. Spain with 10,500,000 and Portugal with nearly 3,000,000 had both grown in population but events were to show that their apparent revival in strength had been illusory.

The most spectacular and far-reaching change was undoubtedly the rise in Russian power—indeed as our perspective lengthens we may see in it the major continental development of the whole century. The ageing Empress Catherine ruled in 1789 over perhaps 30,000,000 people, only about 500,000 of them east of the Urals. The Russian hold on the Baltic had been strengthened by the acquisition of Courland at the time of the first partition of Poland in 1772. The same event had given over to the rule of Moscow, the remainder of White Russia, to the Dvina and Dnieper rivers.

By the Peace of Kutchuk-Kainardji in 1774, Russia acquired the coast of the sea of Azov and the Black Sea littoral between the Dnieper and the Bug, also some rather ill-defined rights of intervention on behalf of Orthodox Christians within the Sultan's domains—right of a kind she had already made good use of in Catholic Poland. The "independence" of the Crimean Tartars was acknowledged by the Turks in the same treaty. This meant that there was no obstacle to Russia's annexation of the peninsula, which was finally acquired at the Peace of Constantinople in 1784. In both 1774 and 1784, renewed advances in the Caspian area were also consolidated; and in the latter year, Russia's suzerainty over Georgia was recognized by the Turks— though it was not until the following century that the resistance of the mountain people was finally broken, so that the way was clear for Joseph Djugashvili, better known as Stalin, to be born a subject of the Tsar.

The Ottoman Empire although the subject of so much spoliation had still a long way to go before it finally disintegrated. Already in 1791 the Ochakov crisis showed that Great Britain regarded itself as concerned to prevent the extension of Russian sovereignty to the point where she might become a Mediterranean power. But Poland, stripped on three sides by the partition of 1772 and cut off from the sea, could get no help from the West. Out of reach of fleets, her fate depended on the three mighty land-powers, Russia, Prussia and Austria. By the further partitions of 1793 and 1795, Poland disappeared from the map as an independent State. The lesson of the period was emphasized again when the Napoleonic revival of the State in the truncated form of the Grand Duchy of Warsaw failed to survive its author's downfall.

Revolutionary France thus faced a Europe in which there were besides herself only four major Powers: Britain, the Empire (Austria), Prussia and Russia. Two of these, Austria and Russia were multinational states, and bound to cling to dynasticism rather than accept the aid against the Revolution, of the newly awakened forces of nationalism.

But the brute facts of area and population that have concerned us in the present chapter do not in themselves explain the vicissitudes of power that have been thus briefly chronicled. Much must be allowed for technical and economic advances. Sweden's temporary importance as an iron-manufacturing country helps to explain the extraordinary seventeenth-century rise of that poor and sparsely populated land. In the eighteenth century, the iron-mines developed under Peter I in the Urals played their part in Russia's rise as a great power. Had Charles VI been successful in revivifying the overseas commerce of Belgium the shifting in the axis of Habsburg power towards the Balkans might have been delayed.

The most important elements of changing strength lay, however, in the twin spheres of administration and finance. Upon these depended the ability of the monarchs to mobilize their nominal power for the stern business of war and diplomacy.

Upon these subjects, the historian of the "Age of Absolutism" must perforce concentrate. And although the fortunes of one country do much to illuminate by comparison and contrast those of the others, enough has been said to show how fundamentally different were the internal problems that they had to face. It is, therefore, more revealing to say something of the individual histories of the major Powers before looking once more at the impact of events that affected and indeed transformed them all.

CHAPTER III

FRANCE

HISTORIANS have no alternative but to accept the common verdict of contemporaries that the central core of European civilization in the age of Louis XIV and his successors was the monarchy of France. As has been suggested, the pre-eminence of France in population and its natural wealth are, no doubt, fundamental to an explanation of this fact. The Wars of Religion and the fragmentation of political authority that resulted from them, had delayed the full exploitation of these advantages. But the tenacious and constructive genius of Cardinal Richelieu had done for Louis XIII what Henry VII of England had largely done for himself more than a century earlier. The rivals of the monarchic power, the old feudal or military nobility and the newer quasi-nobility of the lawyer-caste had failed in their rebellions of the mid-seventeenth century—known as the Fronde—to establish any serious check upon the royal authority. While Charles II of England achieved his restoration only at the price of a permanent shift of power from the Crown to the landed and mercantile aristocracy, Louis XIV found himself at his majority in a position to put into practice those precepts of absolutism that had become common form among political thinkers. The shifts and stratagems that had served Cardinal Mazarin so well during the King's long minority were no longer required; and the prospect of serious internal opposition to royal policies hardly needed to be taken into account.

The secret of the French domination of the European scene was thus very largely political. It was to be found in the respect felt by lesser Princes for one who seemed to have solved the problems of their profession, and to be exploiting them with increasing returns in power and glory. But the reflection of this fact was to be found in the admiration accorded to expressions of the French genius. And as is so often the case, this cultural domination outlived the circumstances that produced it.

The domination of French taste can be traced in architecture and in the visual arts. This was aided by an important emigration of French designers and artists and by the desire of other monarchs to ape the French king in the physical setting of their courtly life as well as in the spirit of their policies. The later endeavours of nationally minded German historians can do little with the unmistakable imprint of France upon Frederick II's palace of Sans-Souci. Ceremony and outward show were so essential and integral a part of eighteenth-century monarchy that to create a Versailles seemed the obvious first step towards acting like its master. The history of art is as essential to a full understanding of eighteenth-century absolutism as the history of political theory, or administrative institutions.

Still more striking was the diffusion of the French language as the normal vehicle of international intercourse, and in many countries as the normal mode of expression of polite society. Latin which had served the former purpose during so many centuries had suffered one blow as a result of the Protestant Reformation. But it was only at the beginning of the eighteenth century that it began, for secular purposes, to be replaced by French. The Treaties of Westphalia were still drawn up in Latin; the Treaty of Rastatt and its successors, in French. Nor was the change for long confined to those treaties in which the French themselves participated. When in 1774, the Russians and Turks negotiated the important treaty of Kutchuk-Kainardji, both sides used French.

Science went the same way as diplomacy. The French published their *Journal des Savants* in the vernacular from 1665, and the use of the French language spread to other countries. In 1743, Frederick II ordered that the publications of the Berlin Academy of Sciences should appear in French, since in his opinion academies to be useful should communicate their discoveries in a universal language. Italy, Spain and Britain resisted this new linguistic hegemony; but in Russia, and elsewhere in eastern and northern Europe its triumph was unequivocal. Indeed Catherine the Great corresponded in

French not only with her eminent French flatterers, Voltaire and Diderot, but even with her fellow-German Grimm. And the great Russian nobles were far more at ease in French than in their native tongue.

If one attaches most importance to language and to the literary forms that went with it, the reason is that this penetration served not only the cause of absolute monarchy, but also that of its critics. It provided a ready means through which ideas critical of the existing social and political systems could be spread throughout Europe from their original forcing-grounds in the literary salons of Paris. The intellectual ascendancy of Voltaire and the "philosophes" and later of Rousseau was facilitated by this general access to the language in which they wrote. Even in so far as the new ideas were of English origin, their diffusion was normally possible only after they had first been taken up in France and assimilated into the body of French writing. Nor perhaps would the vaster and more dangerous currents set in motion by the French Revolution itself have had so great an impact without the preparatory work of intellectual diffusion under the *ancien régime*.

The story of cultural diffusion in this period is not a simple one and has some paradoxical aspects. The expulsion of the French Huguenots after 1685, was for instance, an important factor in the dissemination of scientific ideas. They provided a channel for the entry of French ideas into England and Prussia, and one finds them in Holland editing journals written in French, but drawing for their contents on English ideas as well. The fact of Italian and Spanish resistance to French penetration was of less importance because of the general transfer to the North Sea from the Mediterranean of the cultural centre of the western world. Finally, by creating something in the nature of an international or rather, cosmopolitan culture, the circulation of ideas provided, between the intellectual and social *élites* of the different countries, links of interest and feeling as strong, or in some cases stronger, than those of nationality. This was among the factors that still continued to limit the scope and claims of State action, so long as the *ancien régime* endured. It was no accident that a vociferous claim for the recognition of national cultures and for the rights of national languages—

the ideological aspect of the "romantic movement"—should
have coincided with the democratic onslaught on the institutions of the *ancien régime* itself. It was only then—in the ferment
of the revolutionary and Napoleonic periods—that intellectual
activity became a divisive force and that the states acquired the
habit of utilizing it for their own purposes. Although French
intellectual and artistic leadership was, no doubt, a source of
pride, its conscious exploitation for political purposes in the
eighteenth century is not obvious. The European policy of
France, like that of less strongly based national communities,
was still essentially an affair of the dynasty and its servants.

The brilliance of French thought in the period may have the
effect of leading the historian astray; for the rationale of
monarchical absolutism was more highly developed than its
practice. The idea of sovereignty and hence of the right to
legislate had made progress since the publication in 1576 of
Bodin's *De la République* which some might regard as the
principal text of the new monarchical order. But the arguments
in favour of absolutism to which the Englishman Hobbes had
given a wholly secularist foundation in his *Leviathan* (1651)
were more palatable to the French crown in a religious guise.
And it is to the ecclesiastic Bossuet and to his *Politique Tirée de
l'Ecriture Sainte* (written 1679, and published 1709) that we
must look for an exposition of the foundation in divine
right that Louis XIV claimed for his authority.

But such theories for all their talk of absolute power were
in a sense conservative, since legitimacy was of their essence.
Indeed Bodin explicitly links the monarchical authority to its
obligation to do right; and this meant in effect to respect
private property whether in material possessions, in acquired
rights to office, or in title to social esteem. This limitation
of power by law was not, of course, a novelty, but was a survival
of an older concept of kingship and government. And even
Bossuet's monarch is bound to act within the framework of
the laws, though no power to see that he does so is permitted
to reside in other hands. It was only in the course of the
eighteenth century that political science, like the natural
sciences, began under the impact of a new scepticism to sur-
render the quest for final solutions in favour of the idea of the

enlargement of mental horizons and consequently of technical and social progress. The later theorists of enlightened despotism, Voltaire and the encyclopaedists, were to claim for the monarchy the much wider powers which were necessary if it were to become a real instrument of reform and of change.

By and large, the monarchy of the *ancien régime* remained nevertheless to the end, a conservative force, assisting in the preservation of an extremely hierarchical society which permitted social ascension only along well-marked paths of advancement. It could gradually adapt social institutions to economic change by its legislative or administrative authority, but despite the absolutist claims of its theorists it was relatively powerless when it was a question of directly invading existing privileges, or other vested interests. In other words, the structure of society and the relationships between its various components, and between these and the Crown, were much tougher and less malleable than the theorists of absolutism would have one believe.

These practical limitations on royal power were not without their contemporary institutional expression. The French king's coronation oath to safeguard the liberties of the Church, the traditional situation of the Estates, and to dispense good justice to all, differentiated the lawful monarch from the tyrant of antiquity or the oriental despot. But the King alone represented in his own person the common good of the realm, something distinct from the interests of the social classes, the provinces and corporate bodies of which it was composed. In holding to this view, at any rate in the early part of Louis XIV's reign, the theorists of absolutism had popular sentiment on their side. For the victory over the Fronde seems to have been a popular victory, and the tendency of the masses in France as in other countries so ruled, was to accept the fact that the King was good, and to blame all that went wrong on evil counsel. Nor was the hereditary principle itself subject to challenge. On the contrary, Bossuet could claim it as one of the sources of monarchical strength; for it eliminated the struggles between cliques and factions that characterized the history alike of classical antiquity and of the Hebrews of the Old Testament. It is true that this popular acceptance of the theory and practice of absolutism was not permanent in France. At a given time, as a great French historian has put it; "the majority of Frenchmen think like Bossuet; all of a sudden the French think like Voltaire; it is a revolution". And though Voltaire himself was a monarchist, his critical method could be used to question all existing institutions.

By formal definition, the absolute monarch is one who has limitless means of action and is subject to no control. This latter idea did not, of course, mean in practice that the King took no counsel of others, but simply that his decision was in all cases final. Right up to the eve of the Revolution, the theorists of absolutism held that if there were any organ to which a royal decision could be appealed then that organ, and not the King would be sovereign. By this time such views were not held unanimously. Orthodox theorists held that a "mixed government" like that of England, was not a monarchy at all, but a crowned republic. Others in the eighteenth century, like Montesquieu, preferred the "mixed" to the "pure" monarchy. But this was a preference confined on the whole to the magistrates of the "Parlements" which remained even after the Fronde, the repository of constitutionalist notions. By the eighteenth century, there existed besides the great Parlement of Paris, the jurisdiction of which covered a third of France, twelve provincial Parlements, and four other sovereign courts. Neither in the seventeenth- nor in the eighteenth-century formulations of the monarchical position is there any real trace of a democratic theory of sovereignty. Indeed Bossuet's notion of divine right is less democratic than the typical medieval idea of the way in which power is transmitted from God. For while the medieval thinkers had held that this power could be transmitted through the intermediary of the people, the exploitation of this idea by the advocates of resistance and even of tyrannicide during the Wars of Religion had made it highly suspect; and in Bossuet's scheme of things the royal authority is directly supported by the divine sanction. Nor in his borrowings from Hobbes, did the French writer include the idea of the original contract which was capable of other uses than those which Hobbes had put it to in the interests of absolutism.

So great has been the mental impact of the ideas of abstract and inalienable rights to which the American and French Revolutions gave currency that despite their modern denial in so many quarters, a mental effort is involved in trying to reconstruct the political outlook of a society in whose institutions they found no expression. But it seems clear that the idea of individual rights, the idea of a general liberty, subject only to the condition of refraining from infringing the liberties of others, did not in fact infuse at any point the structure of the French *ancien régime*.

There were rights that were exercised in practice and that were recognized—the right of petition, the right of association for non-political purposes, subject in some cases to official authorization. By the standards of modern totalitarianisms, the France of the eighteenth century was a veritable sanctuary of liberalism. But there was no sanction for such liberties other than usage. And other aspects of the period show a much closer conformity between theory and practice. The *lettres de cachet*, the power of the King to order arrest and imprisonment without trial for an indefinite duration of time at his own pleasure stood out in marked contrast to the entrenchment of *habeas corpus* in English law at the same period—even if this power was normally used only as a sanction for family discipline among the nobility. A similar contrast existed between the relative religious toleration and freedom of the press in England and the French insistence on religious orthodoxy and universal censorship; though here the hold of the government was partially relaxed in the course of the eighteenth century. Even in the fundamental question of property rights, it was undoubtedly true in legal theory that in France, all that belonged to the King's subjects was at his disposal. He could therefore in theory, tax at discretion. It is not in the want of legal authority to tax that we must seek the causes of the defeat of such reformers as Machault, controller-general of finance from 1740 to 1754 and of the ultimate financial failure of the *ancien régime*.

The essential fact is that although the King was subject to no control, he normally acted according to custom and established law. Since the sixteenth century, at any rate, his authority had been regarded as expressing itself in two forms—acts of ordinary or regulated power, and acts of absolute power or

absolute will. It was the same distinction that the early Stuarts
had tried unsuccessfully to establish in England between
"ordinary" and "prerogative" powers.

For the smooth running of the realm, it was imperative that
the monarchy should ordinarily keep to its normal exercise of
its traditional powers. Otherwise it would run up against the
opposition, not of individuals but of organized classes and
groups. For if the rights of the individual were an as yet
unrecognized abstraction, the rights and powers of social groups
were still a formidable force. But it was precisely these groups
that offered the greatest obstacle to any far-reaching changes
in the distribution of wealth, power or esteem, and that were in
the eighteenth century regarded in consequence as an obstacle
to progress. Thus the sole bulwark of liberty against an authority
that might otherwise be crushing was also the principal barrier
to progress—and in this antithesis may perhaps be sought the
real roots of the revolutionary situation that developed with such
speed in the generation preceding 1789. The demand for
individual liberty played in the long run, as we have seen,
straight into the hands of the State, since the State was the
instrument through which the older collective caste or group
liberties were destroyed. And the demand for equality lent
itself with equal facility to the same process. The primary concern of the old corporate groups—aristocratic, professional,
urban or provincial—was to preserve existing inequalities.
That was their *raison d'être*. The slogan of *la carrière ouverte
aux talents*—the most dynamic of the slogans of the French
Revolution—was despite its democratic airs, at the same time
the slogan most suited to the despotic authority of the State.
Indeed the right to choose their servants irrespective of class
and to promote them for merit alone, had been characteristic of
all those monarchs of the past—a Louis XI in France, a
Henry VII in England—who had most impressed their contemporaries with their determination to achieve a genuinely
absolute government.

In the early part of Louis XIV's reign, these developments
were still largely in the future. The system seemed for a time
to have reached a stage of relative equilibrium; the royal power
being sufficiently strong to carry out important policies of

internal improvement and national aggrandizement without degenerating into tyranny, and the various aristocracies retaining enough vitality to provide a healthy circulation in the body politic. Such expressions can be only metaphorical at best; but perhaps they help to convey the situation as it was, and as it may have appeared to contemporaries at a moment when the clouds of civil war and foreign intervention had suddenly and almost miraculously disappeared.

This happy if impermanent state of affairs had been the product of a long and complicated development. By the sixteenth century, the king's power of legislation which had originally been confined to his personal domain alone, was applied to the whole kingdom and limited, apart from divine and natural law, only by the fundamental laws of the kingdom: those governing the succession making it the appanage of a family not of an individual, and establishing the inalienability of the domain. In view of Henry IV's conversion, it might be argued that the succession to the French throne was governed not merely by the principle of descent through males only, but also by the principle that the monarch must be a Catholic. The Kings could not change the order of succession. In 1717, an edict of Louis XIV giving his legitimated sons a place in the order of succession was declared void. The luck of the dynasty prevented any test of whether the succession could be broken by the voluntary renunciation of its beneficiaries. The birth of a dauphin to Louis XV meant that Philip V of Spain, who had renounced his rights in France by the Treaty of Utrecht, was anyhow no longer the heir. The efforts of the Parlements, and especially of the Parlement of Paris, after 1753, to use their right of registering laws in order to constitute themselves the guardians of an assumed body of traditional law that could not be altered or abrogated by the royal fiat was a highly controversial one, and has, by some historians, been regarded as frankly revolutionary.

As far as private law was concerned, it was normal for the Crown to respect the whole vast body of such law that was still determined by local custom. But even in this sphere, the royal legislative power could be called in where custom seemed to run contrary to public policy. In the sphere of public law—in all that related to the estates or classes into which the people were divided and in all that related to the machinery of justice and of government—the activity of the monarch was necessarily incessant. If the machine were left alone too long—so experience seemed to prove—abuses always crept in. Delegated power was always turned to private profit. Reform was only possible from above. In the Middle Ages and in the sixteenth century, such reform had often at least, been undertaken in conjunction with the representatives of the estates themselves, assembled in the States-General.

But the pretensions of the nobility during the Wars of Religion had rendered this institution much disliked by the Crown and its servants. By the time of Louis XIV's majority, it was a generation since the States-General had met, and it was not revived. Nevertheless, under both Louis XIV and his successor, there was a good deal of legislative activity which amounted at times to a sustained effort at codification. Modern historians of French law still point to the importance in civil procedure of the code of 1667, and in criminal procedure, to the code of 1670.

The notion of Estates did not, however, disappear with the desuetude of the machinery for their representation. Indeed when such representation was felt necessary in 1789, it was the old model that was revived, even though it did not long survive in its traditional form, and was soon forced to accept the new individualistic climate by transmuting itself into a national assembly. The distinction between the two terms is a measure of the distance France had travelled. It was a prime task of the Revolution to turn the French nation into a single collectivity, divided for administrative purposes, and for administrative purposes only into the utilitarian and deliberately unhistorical divisions of departments and cantons.

But in 1660, Rousseau and the results of his teachings that were thus to be exemplified, were still far in the future; and France presented to the observer an almost indescribably complex series of class and territorial divisions. The division by Estates was by far the simplest. Every Frenchman unless he was a serf—and serfdom by the eve of the Revolution came to be a mere local survival, accounting for perhaps 1,000,000 souls out of a population of 25,000,000—was either a noble, or a member of the clergy, or the Third Estate. In addition to the Estates, there were the corporate bodies, the chapters of cathedrals and abbeys, the monastic orders, the universities and academies, and the various professional officials, judicial, administrative and fiscal, welded by the system of purchasable and hereditary offices into a very distinctive element in the body politic. Of almost equal significance were the territorial divisions—the "pays" or provinces. Their existence reflected the long and turbulent history by which successive dynasties had built up the French monarchy round the original nucleus of the Ile de France. In some cases linguistic differences still recalled their previous separate existence. The royal ordinances still talked of the king's peoples rather than of his people; and where provinces had been recently annexed their peculiarities in laws and customs were upheld. The same was true of the privileges of the towns, where the King in many cases replaced the feudal seigneur from whom they had first won the right of independent organization and limited self-government. This involved accepting the rôle of the various corporate bodies within the towns which provided the basis for their municipal institution. The same respect was shown to the institutions of the various cities of the Empire that fell to France in the sixteenth and seventeenth centuries—Metz, Toul, Verdun, Cambrai and Strasbourg. All such territorial divisions had a legal existence, even when they had no politically representative organs. But those provinces that had retained their own Estates The *Pays d'Etats* were privileged by comparison with the *Pays d'Elections* where no such assemblies existed.

On the whole the *Pays d'Etats* in the eighteenth century, were the acquisitions on the periphery of the kingdom, Flanders, Artois, Britanny, Navarre, Béarn and the other smaller Pyrenean provinces, Languedoc, Burgundy and Provence. Other Estates which had existed were by now dormant. Where the Estates survived, they gave the province concerned a certain position of privilege as against the rest of France. When the country was subjected to a new tax, they voted a "voluntary gift" instead. The Estates, and not the royal administration, were responsible for the assessment and

levying of the individual contributions: to some extent, they
could budget directly for local matters—canals, ports, roads and
charitable and scientific purposes. Their credit unlike that of
the Central Government remained high until the Revolution.
The municipalities were increasingly subjected to royal
control. It came to be assumed by the government that such
powers as they possessed were simply delegated from the Crown.
The element of self-government in their institutions was pro-
gressively weakened, particularly after the system began in the
last decade of the seventeenth century, of extending to the
mayoralty and other municipal offices, the practice of purchase.
Through the intendant, there was a close interaction between
governmental and municipal powers; and one finds municipalities held responsible for assessing taxes, supervising the draw
for the militia and for billeting troops. There was never any
question of the French towns becoming virtual republics like
the cities of the Empire. What was true of their laws was true
of all local and special laws, and of the rules of all corporations
and professional organizations; the royal power was the
ultimate sanction and their authority derived from the assumption that they had its support.
    Although the towns were in a sense administrative units, the
historic provinces were not. Each province whether or not it
had its own Estates, had indeed its laws, customs and traditions
and perhaps its local speech. But administration ignored
it. The judicial and therefore administrative units were
the ancient bailiwicks and seneschalships; were above them
the seventeenth-century "generalities". In addition there were
the ecclesiastical provinces and dioceses, the military governorships and commands, and the judicial divisions, including the
areas of competence of the several Parlements. At no point did
the boundaries of these different types of division coincide.
    By far the most important division was the generality which
formed the sphere of activity of the intendant, the key
personality of the whole local administrative system. There were
generalities which coincided with provinces—as was the case in
Brittany, Languedoc and Provence. But some provinces were
sub-divided into generalities, like Normandy which had three;
some generalities were formed by joining provinces together.

Altogether in 1789, there were thirty-two generalities—units too large for efficiency in the opinion of many would-be reformers and certainly much larger than the counties which were the units for the very much less intensive local government of England. But their extent and functions were at least clearly defined which was more than could be said for the heterogeneous and confused jumble of subordinate divisions wherein the spirit of local particularism and conservatism could most easily find support. The neat formulae of absolutism take on a new aspect when considered under this light.

Earlier kings had been obliged to reckon with the possible opposition of both Church and nobility. The former relationship had been complicated in the sixteenth century by the emergence of French Protestantism, with for a time important backing, both socially and territorially. The concessions made to it by the Edict of Nantes had almost created a State within a State. But in the course of the century, this position had been whittled away to the point where Louis XIV could safely dispense with the Edict. The great majority of the people had been won back to the Catholic fold; and the tradition of dissent was substantially driven underground. But the dominant Church found that the monarchy was strong enough to insist upon its own interpretation of the proper relations between itself and the Papacy. And as events in the reign of Louis XIV himself showed, opposition to the royal wishes might result in schism. In the latter part of his reign, the monarch's increasing sensibility to the clerical influences represented by Madame de Maintenon whom he married in 1684, led him to throw the royal power heavily on the side of orthodoxy against Jansenism, and thus to add yet another undercurrent to the future tides of opposition to the whole absolutist system. Only the dissolution of the Jesuit order in France in 1764 finally ended the Jansenist controversy itself.

On its side, the Church, while closely linked to the monarchy, did nevertheless preserve some important privileges particularly in the sphere of taxation, which was of great importance in view of the extent of the Church's landed property. The origins of the eighteenth-century system go back to the sixteenth-century bargain between the Church and the Crown, whereby the clergy got both the royal protection for their lands in face of the covetousness of a nobility stimulated by the spectacle of the plunder opened to their class in Protestant countries, and also immunity from the ordinary forms of taxation. In return the Church paid a single block grant voted by a Church Assembly called every ten years. The grant consisted partly of the sum fixed at the time when such grants were first made, and partly of subsequent additions to it. Every time ordinary taxation was increased, the Church purchased its immunity by the promise of an additional grant. Under this system, the clergy got off relatively lightly in peacetime but was called upon for heavy "voluntary contributions" in time of war. In assessing the proportion of the Church's contribution to the national expenditure in relation to its own wealth, it has to be borne in mind that in what were known as the *pays conquis*, that is to say those territories added to France since the original bargain— Flanders, Artois, Hainaut, the Cambrésis, Lorraine, Alsace, Franche-Comté and Roussillon—where about a quarter of the wealth of the Church actually lay, this system did not operate. There the clergy either paid the ordinary taxes— *vingtièmes* and *capitation* like the nobles, or compounded specially. On the whole there would seem to be good grounds for taking the view that the Church escaped from part of the burden that the State could have claimed the right to impose. It justified this position which it retained right up until the Revolution by the claim that it was performing out of its own revenues services of a charitable and social nature that might otherwise have fallen to the share of the public authorities. But the wealth of the Church remained a potent source of anti-clerical incitement.

The successful resistance of the Church to attacks upon it in sixteenth-century France meant as its obverse, a failure on the part of the nobility. The French secular landowners did not like their English counterparts get compensation for their losses through the price-revolution, by receiving an increment of Church lands. And their economic weakness, as well as the general weariness provoked by the wars of religion, must have assisted in the task of taming them. They discovered under Richelieu that their loss of local control could not be made up for by a veto on government at the centre. By the end of the fifteenth century, France had avoided the fate of Germany: she was to be a single country, not a jumble of independent jurisdictions. By the middle of the seventeenth century she had shown that she was not to be a Poland either.

Nevertheless this weakness of the French nobility was relative, not absolute. It remained an important and closely knit class, entrenched in law as well as in esteem, and prepared to struggle for the retention of its privileges. Its numerical strength is hard to calculate; Vauban in the latter part of Louis XIV's reign reckoned it at 200,000 or about 1 per cent of the population. Another survey, on the eve of the Revolution, gave the number as only 78,000. Whichever figure one accepts, the reality of the problem it presented cannot be denied.

Impeded by law from indulging in industrial and commercial occupations though not from emigration to the colonies, its younger sons could not provide a bridge with the business world like that which characterized the English scene. And even when such legislation was modified as it was in 1765, the prejudices of caste were too strong for the openings to be taken. Since the Crown suspected the nobility too much to employ it in the civil administration, to any large extent, its only fields of action were the army and the church. In peacetime, the French aristocracy was confronted with two unpalatable alternatives—either to waste its substance living at Court and living up to the increasingly luxurious standards that Versailles demanded—or if this was out of the question, to reside obscurely on the family estates, cut off from the fountain of honour and of profit.

In such circumstances, the vested interest of the nobility in a large army, and in an army of a particular kind is easy enough to understand. The nobles naturally insisted upon commissions for their offspring at an early age; and it was in consequence hard to insist that they got adequate training before they became officers in their fourteenth or fifteenth year. Between 1682 and 1692, special cadet companies were set up to train them. But Louis XIV dissolved these after the death of his great war minister Louvois; and although another attempt on the same lines was made between 1726 and 1733 it was unsuccessful. In 1751, the Ecole Militaire was founded for the impecunious sons of the French nobles, on the initiative of the financier and war-profiteer Pâris-Duverney. This at first made little improvement; but in 1776 it was reorganized as a higher military academy open to the best graduates of the provincial military colleges—the young Bonaparte entered it from Brienne in 1784—and began to meet the need for more advanced military training.

The composition and nature of the army was also affected by another factor for which the existence of a privileged and under-taxed nobility was partly responsible, the financial weakness of the Crown itself. The creation and sale of new military posts was a common expedient. In 1702, Louis XIV created 7,000 officers' commissions; and a few years later there were as many officers receiving pensions as on the active list. The increasing tendency of commissions to fall to the sons of the new plutocracy of the eighteenth century appeared as a threat to the aristocracy's important monopoly. And it was this objection to the increasing social weight of commercial wealth, rather than objection to the principle of promotion from the ranks, that brought about the decree of 1781, by which the military schools were closed to all those of insufficiently aristocratic stock. In the same pre-Revolutionary decades the *noblesse de robe* of the Parlements also took steps to limit access to them to those possessing hereditary membership of their caste.

Nevertheless, the army list continued to be inflated. In 1787, the French army contained 36,000 officers all drawing pay, but with only 13,000 on active duty. Something like two-thirds of these on the active list were nobles. The commoners were, of course, primarily to be found in the technical arms where more specialized training was essential. The number of generals was also too large. There were over 1,100 of them in the French army on the eve of the Revolution, compared with only eighty in the rather larger army of Prussia. Finally, the officer-corps revealed the considerable cleavage within the territorial aristocracy itself. All commissions above those of lieutenant had to be bought; so that an officer from the petty country nobility, or squirearchy as it should perhaps be called, could hardly get his foot above the first rung of the ladder.

On the other hand, the higher positions normally went to the great court families who had access to the sources of patronage.

It has often been pointed out that by accepting the continuation of their privileges, after they had ceased to perform most of the social functions that justified them, the French aristocracy sealed its own doom. But it is never easy for members of a social class to see any alternative way of life to that which they have traditionally followed; and even the historian with the benefit of knowing what was to come may find it hard to suggest what other course lay open. Certainly, the French nobles were by the middle of the seventeenth century, incompetent as a class to undertake political responsibilities. It only required an opportunity for them to make this plain. Both during the minority of Louis XIV and after his death, at the time of the so-called aristocratic reaction under the regency of the Duke of Orleans, the nobility had power in their hands, and showed that they had no idea how to use or consolidate it. They had neither the legal nor the economic information necessary. They could neither identify themselves whole-heartedly with the State, nor acquire the habit of daily devotion to bureaucratic routine which was the foundation of the power of the great servants of the monarchy such as Colbert and Louvois. All the schemes of Fénelon, Saint-Simon, Chevreuse and the rest, collapsed on the rock of this essential fact.

The conditions after Louis XIV's death were, of course, exceptional. After his seizure of sole power in agreement with the Parlement of Paris, but in defiance of Louis XIV's testaments, the Regent reversed the monarchy's habit of governing through individual ministers separately responsible, in favour of a system of Councils—the so-called *polysynodie*. The fact that they were primarily composed of nobles is sufficient to explain their failure. The Regent was forced to rule through a virtual Prime Minister—the Abbé Dubois. Following the financial collapse associated with the experiments of John Law and the Regent's death in 1723, Cardinal Fleury went back to the old system. When he died, twenty years later, Louis XV ruled in theory as Louis XIV had done, without a first minister, which meant a process of balancing one minister against another, with the King having often, a policy of his own, particularly in foreign affairs. Nevertheless, the royal government was strong enough for the King utterly to defeat a new attempt by the Parlements to get their unhistorical claim to political authority accepted. It was only when the problem of paying for the American war brought about the crisis of the reign of Louis XVI that the structure of monarchical power could seriously be assailed.

When it fell, the privileges of the aristocracy fell with it; and this suggests that, despite the apparent existence of an intermittent conflict between the Crown and the nobility, there was a deeper sense in which their interests were linked. This fact was perceived by Montesquieu and other eighteenth-century writers; and the action of the Crown in supporting the privileges of the nobility even while thwarting its political ambitions is evidence enough that even an absolutist monarch could not visualize his position as other than that of the coping-stone of a caste society.

In the organization of government, the Crown had to deal with the claim of the great nobles to be the natural counsellors of the monarch, and as such to figure in his Council. The system perfected by Louis XIV was to meet this by differentiating between the functions of the different types of session of what was still in form a single body, the Conseil d'Etat du Roi. That this had in fact come to be a fiction is attested by the fact that the common usage was to talk of "councils" in the plural. It is, indeed, possible to follow the modern practice and to differentiate between councils concerned with government, in the sense of high matters of policy, and councils concerned with justice and administration.

In Louis XIV's reign there were three councils of the former kind, all of which the King attended in person. There was the Conseil d'Etat sometimes known as the Conseil d'en Haut because held on the upper floor of the palace of Versailles near the King's own apartment, and sometimes referred to as the Conseil Secret. It consisted of five or six important persons, known as the Ministers of State, who normally included the Secretaries of State for foreign affairs, the army and the navy and the Controller-General of finance. In addition one or two important nobles or Marshals might be present. The essential point was that members were invited separately for each session, so that anyone could be dropped at any time at the sole will of the King. It could, therefore, never consolidate itself into an institution on its own. It dealt with all the major matters of State, and in particular with foreign affairs, holding normally in Louis XIV's reign, three long sessions a week.

Internal government, the supervision of the administration and of the courts and of the various corporate bodies rested with the Conseil des Depêches which met fortnightly. Here the King was joined by the Ministers of State, by the Chancellor, by those Secretaries of State who did not hold the exalted rank of Ministers of State, and by one or two of the legal advisers known as Councillors of State. This was the body that dealt with the affair of the Parlements in the reign of Louis XV.

The Conseil Royal des Finances was created in 1661 after the disgrace of the once all-powerful Fouquet when the King decided that it would be safer to abolish altogether the great office of Superintendent of Finance. It included the Chancellor, a highly paid officer known as the Chef du Conseil Royal des Finances (often a Marshal), the Controller-General of finance and two Intendants of Finance as well as two senior Councillors of State. Its weekly meetings dealt with all matters regarding the levying of taxes and the royal domains and with all legal disputes arising out of financial questions.

Meanwhile the sessions of the Council dealing with Justice and Administration had been since 1624 grouped apart under the designation of, Conseil d'Etat Privé, finances et direction. It was here that the Peers retained their right to sit alongside the Ministers and Secretaries of State. But in fact the work was done by the permanent officials attached to the Council. After a reorganization in 1673, these consisted of thirty councillors. Three of these were from the clergy and three were nobles, but the remainder were drawn from the hereditary official and legal class—although these councillors were, strictly speaking, "commissaires" not "officiers" that is to say although they held their offices by nomination not as of right, or by purchase, they were in fact guaranteed independence and permanence. And their functions led on to the attainment of the highest offices, those of Minister or Ambassador. Another eighty officials

known as Masters of Requests, who formally belonged to the
royal household, and not to the council and who had other
duties, were nevertheless available for the council to call upon.
These posts were open to purchase and at a high price; their
holders belonged socially to the upper bourgeoisie, and the
position served as a jumping-off ground for ambitious young
men.

The system retained flexibility, since the underlying assumption that the King could always consult anyone he wished to,
enabled further councils to be set up when needed within the
original framework. Thus there was the Conseil de Conscience
in which the King and his confessor dealt with ecclesiastical
appointments. And after 1700 there was the Conseil de Commerce. Alongside this, there functioned a Bureau de Commerce
which could summon to its deliberations, representatives of the
municipal chambers of commerce.

Since it was important to keep alive the notion of the
unity of the Council, its business whether emanating from the
various departments of State, or through petitions, from private
citizens or corporate bodies, was addressed to it as a whole.
It was the special function of the Chancellor, assisted by a
series of offices and committees staffed by councillors or
masters of requests, to sort out the different matters and direct
them through the proper channels. One may suppose that such
functions gave to these bodies much of the power that
secretariats of this kind normally tend to acquire.

Under the experiment of the *polysynodie*, the Regency
Council replaced the Conseil d'en Haut. Seven other specialized
councils were created to deal with the different aspects of
government: ecclesiastical affairs; foreign affairs; war; navy;
finance; internal affairs; commerce. Each was presided over
by a Prince of the Blood or some other great noble, and was
composed of nobles and of councillors of State. Instead of
business going through the office of the Secretaries of State,
it went direct to the President of the relevant council. The
Council after discussing the matter made a proposal to the
Regent who settled it personally or submitted it to the Council
of Regency. This reduced the Secretaries of State, who were
frowned upon as Louis XIV's bureaucratic upstarts, to the level

of mere executants. But in spite of the successes of two of these councils, that of finance under the Duc de Noailles, and that of the navy under the Comte de Toulouse (son of Louis XIV and Madame de Montespan), the system as a whole made too great demands upon the assiduity of the nobles; and, as has been seen, it did not long survive.

But the old system never worked again as smoothly as under Louis XIV. Particularly in the latter half of the eighteenth century, it was clear that government by Council was breaking down. The ministers of the Crown and in particular the Controller-General were unwilling to put up with the intervention of the offices and committees of the Council. They dealt directly with the King on matters which could usefully have gone before it, and secured from the King and the Chancellor, decrees of the Council that had never in fact been before that body in proper sessions. In as far as they took advice, it was from consultative bodies within their own departments. And while the power of ministers increased, departmental co-ordination lagged.

Some of the change was due to the increasing volume of official business; but much of it must be put down to the personal characteristics of the kings. Louis XV held his Councils regularly but found them boring, and let his ministers hold informal meetings between themselves to predigest the business. Normally, he accepted what they did, but occasionally created confusion by going behind their backs. Louis XVI, though more industrious was unintelligent and lent himself to the views of successive ministers, having few opinions of his own except on matters of foreign policy. The defenders of absolutism had traditionally argued that an hereditary monarch was the best kind of ruler; because he would never be able to separate the public weal from the interest of his dynasty and would serve it, if only in order that the glory might rebound to the benefit of himself and his descendants. What they had not considered was that a mere intention to govern well would not be sufficient. The modern state also demanded competence and assiduity; these the hereditary principle failed to provide. Thus Louis XVI reversed the policy of Maupeou's reforming ministry in the last four years of his predecessor's reign, and restored the

Parlements which had been dissolved or set aside, in order to crush their opposition to it. The failure of the monarchical principle was the more marked because of the fact that on its purely judicial and administrative side where the monarch was not personally involved, the machinery of the Council worked well right up to the fall of the regime. Indeed French historians discern its imprint upon the organization of the modern Conseil d'Etat.

The word "ministers" itself does not appear in France, in the modern sense in which we have been using it until the middle of the eighteenth century, and in official language, not until the reign of Louis XVI. The idea itself was also slow to develop. In the Middle Ages when Royal Household and Government were even more indistinguishable than in the reign of Louis XIV, there were the great officers of the Crown— the Seneschal, the Constable and so on—whose court functions were hardly distinguishable from their public ones.

By the seventeenth century, the tendency was for the holders of these posts to be confined to ceremonial duties as a part of the general process of removing the great nobles from all positions of power. After 1627, the office of Constable was abolished and Louis XIV refused to revive it in favour of Marshal Villars after the latter's victory at Denain in 1712 which saved France from invasion. Of the great officers indeed only the Chancellor survived into the age of absolutism; and it was from his entourage that were drawn the typical agents of absolutism, the Secretaries of State.

The Ministers of State of the seventeenth and eighteenth centuries were the members of the Conseil d'en Haut. The Controller-General was usually a Minister of State, and the same was true sometimes of one of the Secretaries and of the Chancellor.

There was usually no formal order of importance between the Ministers of State. Richelieu had been called first minister unofficially, and Mazarin was actually given that title. But in 1661, Louis XIV declared that he wanted no first minister. In fact, the senior member of the Conseil d'en Haut, Michel le Tellier, the Secretary of State for war, was commonly called first minister. Thereafter the designation disappeared until it was revived for the Abbé Dubois, and after his death for the Duke of Orleans. Neither the Duke of Bourbon, who acted as principal minister between 1723 and 1726, nor his successor, Cardinal Fleury ever took the title; and after the death of the latter in 1743, the function itself disappeared again, since the King ordered the principal ministers, the so-called "Committee", the Controller-General Orry, and the Secretaries of State for the navy, for war and for foreign affairs, Maurepas, d'Argenson, and Amelot to report directly to himself.

When Louis XVI came to the throne in 1774, Maurepas who had long been in disgrace was given as senior Minister of State what were virtually the powers of a First Minister. And the title itself was once more revived for Loménie de Brienne in 1787-8. Thus of the great servants of the Crown neither Colbert nor Louvois, nor Choiseul were ever first ministers; they all held office in periods when the Secretaries reported directly to the King, whereas it was the mark of a first minister that all matters should first be handled by himself. The use of the word ministry as it is found in France in the eighteenth century denotes no kind of collective responsibility; it is simply the name given to a number of important persons, appointed by the King and individually responsible to him; its essential nucleus consists of the Chancellor, the four Secretaries of State and the Controller-General of finance. The heads of certain other services, who had the right of direct access to the King, might also be considered as ministers of a kind, at this time. They were the superintendent of buildings who exercised a general responsibility in the field of arts and letters; the superintendent of fortifications, an office made illustrious under Louis XIV by the great Vauban; the secretary of the Council of Conscience, and the Lieutenant-General of the Paris police. The separation of the Court from Paris, and the tendency for the great city to be the focus of all forms of opposition in a century when the urban mob was a greater factor in politics than ever before or since, made the last post one of great importance.

Precedence among the senior personages went to the Chancellor who was in theory and practice irremovable, as had been the case with the holders of all the great household posts. His technical function of sealing all the royal documents

gave him the right to advise on their contents. He was responsible for the drafting of legislation, and had in addition the
formidable rôle of press censor. He supervised the judicial and
administrative aspects of the Council's work, and the Courts of
Law, and was the intermediary between the Crown and the
Parlements; all these when also Garde des Sceaux.

The four secretaryships had been established under
Richelieu. Each Secretary of State was responsible for one
principal department—the royal household, foreign affairs,
the navy and war. Other less important functions were distributed between them in ways which varied from time to time.
But in addition to the functional organization, there was also a
territorial one, since each Secretary was responsible for a certain
number of provinces. The Secretary for War had to look after
the frontier provinces, and the Secretary for the Navy after
certain maritime ones, whence ships and men were drawn. The
importance of the French connexion with the Levant led to
Provence falling to the care of the Secretary for Foreign
Affairs. Although Marseilles which had a veritable monopoly
of such commerce was relatively less important in the eighteenth
than in the seventeenth century, because of the general upsurge
of French overseas commerce, France remained the predominant
country in the trade with the Levant, and exercised a corresponding influence at the Turkish court. The remaining
provinces fell to the Secretary for the Household whose other
duties were less arduous than those of his colleagues.

Eighteenth-century reformers concerned with the efficiency
of the Government, particularly in economic matters, such as
Malesherbes and Turgot, agitated for the creation of a special
post of Secretary for the Interior; but this post was not created
until after the Revolution. A fifth secretaryship was actually
created in 1771. It was held by Bertin, previously Controller-
General, who from 1761 to 1783 was under various titles a
virtual minister of economic affairs. But the extra secretaryship
itself was abolished in 1780.

It is, of course, inseparable from the general ideas underlying the whole system of government that despite this depart-
mentalization the primary duty of all Secretaries was still that of
attending upon the King and of giving expression to his

declared wishes in written form. All documents not of such formality as to require the Chancellor's seal had to be countersigned by a Secretary of State, as well as signed by the King. Even in the case of unimportant documents a facsimile of the royal signature was necessary.

The Secretaries of State were normally recruited from among the Councillors of State. They thus stood at the apex of the *noblesse de robe*, the hereditary nobility drawn from the Parlements and the royal Council which by the eighteenth century came to rival the older feudal nobility, and which by its wealth and by intermarriage became almost indistinguishable from it. There were veritable dynasties of Secretaries of State: Villeroi, Brienne, Colbert, Le Tellier, Phelypeaux, although the habit of conferring separate titles tends to obscure this fact. By the middle of the eighteenth century, the importance of these posts made them coveted even by members of the feudal nobility, the older *noblesse d'epée*: Choiseul, Ségur, d'Aiguillon.

After the disgrace of Fouquet at the beginning of Louis XIV's personal rule, the finances of the kingdom were run by the King in his royal council of finance. It was here that the great figure of Colbert emerged; and he was made Controller-General of Finance in 1665. The position did not correspond with that of the old Superintendent, because the King retained for himself the right of authorizing all expenditure; but it was a very important one and remained so throughout the *ancien régime*. Colbert set the pattern for his successors by treating his fiscal responsibilities in the wider context of general economic policy. In the following century, the Secretary of State d'Argenson, whose father had been Controller-General, wrote that the Controller-General had two functions "that of intendant of the treasury and that of minister of interior affairs of the kingdom". Elsewhere he refers to him as "minister of finances and of the interior". Towards the end of the period, the title of Minister of Finance is in current use.

The Controllers-General came into their office from two very different kinds of beginning. Most of them were already Crown servants, either intendants that is to say provincial governors, like the reformer Turgot or intendants of finance such as Colbert himself. The intendants of finance together with the intendants of commerce, both drawn from among the councillors of State, formed the most important element in the Controller-General's department. But two celebrated finance ministers of the eighteenth century came to the office from private business. One was the Scottish adventurer and projector, John Law who became a Catholic in order to be qualified for the office of Controller-General, which he held 1719–20, before his "bubble" burst. The other was the Swiss banker Necker, whose obstinate protestantism prevented him from holding the office itself though he exercised its functions on two occasions with the title of Director-General. In his case it is hard to keep his private and his public capacities apart. In 1778, during his first term of office he lent the Government 2,000,000 livres from his personal fortune. This was still unpaid at the time of the Revolution and despite the efforts of his celebrated daughter Madame de Staël, his family did not recover it until the reign of Louis XVIII.

The system of which these functionaries were the heads, presupposed an efficient bureaucracy which could both carry through major inquiries and see to the execution of the policies that resulted from them. The origin of the system can be traced back into the later Middle Ages, but its essential features date from the sixteenth century. From that time onwards, the bulk of the Crown's servants can be divided into two major categories, the "commissaires" and the "officiers". The essential differences between them lay in the system of recruitment and tenure.

The commissaries held their positions in virtue of royal commissions nominating them individually to their posts, and informing the public of their functions and powers in a precise fashion. Sometimes the commissions included a limitation as to time or place; but in any event they were revocable by the King, though only he could restrain the commissaries in the event of their exceeding their powers. Their numbers varied and tended to increase in times of trouble. When a position acquired permanence it could be turned into an ordinary office —*office formé*—but this too could be gone back upon. There is thus a certain oscillation between commissary and officer, but in the latter half of the eighteenth century, the tendency is towards multiplying the former. The new functions of government of the period—those of the bridge and road engineering corps for instance—are performed by commissaries.

The principal posts were always held on these revocable terms: all diplomatic and most military ones and those of Secretary of State, Keeper of the Seals, Controller-General, Councillors of State, Governors, Intendants, Intendants of Finance, and Presidents of Parlements. But the division was not quite firm; for there existed through the purchase of reversions or survivorships the possibility of giving such posts the hereditary and venal character that was characteristic of offices. It was in this way that the dynasties of Secretaries of State were formed. Indeed, Le Tellier as Secretary for War obtained the right for his son Louvois to succeed him as early as 1655 when the latter was only fifteen years old, though this reversion did not take effect for another eleven years. Such transactions did not obstruct the royal right of dismissal; but if a reversion had been bought the Crown had to repay the money spent on it if the post was not forthcoming. In fact, in the case of most of the commissaries—men such as councillors of State or intendants—dismissal was rare.

The officers were much more numerous than the commissaries in the seventeenth and eighteenth centuries, and account for the vast majority of posts in the courts, and in financial and administrative organs, both central and local. Offices were created by edicts that specified the functions attached to them. Thus when an appointment was made, it was necessary only to name the appointee, and identify the office. Such appointments were made by letters of provision registered with the sovereign courts. Hence the holders were only removable for grave causes, judicially determined. The King could, of course, suppress an office altogether if it were no longer useful; but in that case he was obliged to compensate the holder for the loss of his rights. The officers would thus seem to correspond to the modern professional civil servant; what distinguishes the two are the twin practices of venality and heredity—practices by no means confined to France.

In the Middle Ages, offices had been sold by their holders

to new aspirants, although the tacit consent of the King was necessary. The idea of creating offices for the purpose of selling them seems to have originated with French municipalities in the fourteenth century, since they found this method of raising revenue preferable to the imposition of taxes. By the end of the fifteenth century, the monarchy had succumbed to their example. In 1522, a special branch of the treasury was set up to deal with revenues from this source. In the case of existing offices, their holders continued to sell them but part of the proceeds came into the treasury. What the officers found still more desirable was to make their posts hereditary in their own families. It was sometimes possible to get the King to recognize a right of inheritance; but not always; and the King could always revoke his consent. To resign in favour of one's son in one's own lifetime was also possible; but as with resignations in favour of those to whom a reversion had been sold, it was necessary to do this at least forty days before the holder of the post died; and this was clearly awkward, while exemptions from the rule though obtainable were expensive.

It was not until 1604 that this problem was solved by an institution known after its projector, Charles Paulet. The *paulette* was a tax of one-sixtieth upon all offices. In return for this payment, the treasury's share of the selling-price was reduced and the rights of heirs guaranteed. There were originally some objections raised—from the nobles in the States-General of 1614, since it weakened the position of would-be patrons, and from the Parlements in the Fronde in 1648—but after temporary suspensions, the *paulette* was restored; and by the second half of the seventeenth century, the whole system was a thoroughly accepted part of France's institutions. The fact that it applied to quite minor governmental posts made it as acceptable to the lowest stratum of the bourgeoisie as to their social superiors.

It will thus be seen that the letters of provision nominating to an office were in the eighteenth century, normally made out in favour of candidates who had already acquired a legal right to the post in question. It was still possible for the King to refuse a particular candidate if he lacked the necessary technical qualifications, such as the proper degrees, and in very special

cases, the "owner" of the office could be made to sell it to a
royal nominee. But the notion of private property in an office
was unimpaired.

From the point of view of the Crown, the main advantages
of the system were fiscal. The King could sell new offices and
received an income from existing ones. In times of stringency,
holders of existing offices could be made to buy increases in
their own salaries, or to buy up newly created ones. In fact, the
Crown was thus obtaining from its own servants what were
really forced loans at a rate of interest very advantageous to the
borrower. Indeed, so high did the price of offices become and so
low were the salaries attached, that in the end little but prestige
was purchased.

As a result of this system access to the higher offices was
attainable only by the rich. And it might take several generations for a family to get to the top of the official tree. Some
offices carried a personal title of nobility and some an hereditary
one; so there was no limit to ambition. Montesquieu's defence
of the system as one inspiring industry is, therefore, not without
foundation, and there is a genuine element of common sense in
his view that the monarch will get no worse servants by trusting
to chance than he would if he were to choose them himself. A
certain element of continuity in administration was provided
and it was a guarantee of the independence of the magistracy.
So long as it existed it meant that service to the State was
considered honourable. But it had its dangers. It turned
ambition away from more adventurous fields such as economic
enterprise. And when new offices were created for financial
reasons, the process impoverished those who were forced to buy
them. In other words it was from the economist's viewpoint an
unproductive form of capital investment. Furthermore, it
helped to consolidate the caste spirit of the official class and in
particular of the parlementaires; and even when their claims
to political power had been repulsed, their very existence was a
stimulus to social radicalism.

The complexities of the social system and the resistance
of its privileged elements to change were most emphatically
demonstrated in the sphere of finance. The finances of the
ancien régime remained until the Revolution itself in a state

of confusion and the financial embarrassments of the Crown continued to grow with every new recourse to war. By 1789, the interest on the national debt alone was more than half the total expenditure and the annual deficit was not less than one fifth of the budget.

The taxes themselves were many and vexatious—though their number and vexatiousness was more striking to historians writing a generation ago than they seem today. The principal tax was the *taille* which was paid by commoners only. Its assessment varied in different regions, being either paid by individuals according to the external indications of their capacity to pay, or as a land-tax. The absence of a proper land-survey or register made all land-taxes highly arbitrary in their incidence, particularly in a period of important agricultural development such as set in from the middle of the eighteenth century. The *capitation* was theoretically a general poll-tax; but the clergy as has been seen compounded for it; and the nobility paid much less in proportion to their wealth than strict equality would have demanded. Thus the burden of this tax, too, fell on the common people. The same was true of the *vingtièmes*, a kind of income tax; for here, too, the clergy had compounded and the nobility paid little. Officials and pensioners had the tax deducted at source. In addition to the three direct taxes, there were a large number of indirect taxes including both external and internal customs: the *aides*, the excise on wine and other drinks and the much detested *gabelle* or salt-tax, the variations of which between the different provinces gave rise to much internal smuggling.

The productivity of the indirect taxes was much less impressive than the burden on the community which they represented, since their collection was farmed-out, and a great deal of the actual income from them remained in the pockets of the tax-farmers. It has indeed been calculated that by 1789 about 60 per cent of the gross revenue never reached the treasury at all. The failure of the monarchy to dispense with the tax-farmers—a failure which grew out of their inability to find any other source for the loans with which to anticipate their deficient revenues—was indeed of great significance. As will be seen, the problem of national credit was not one that troubled the French monarchy alone; but it represents a striking contrast to the imposing apparatus of borrowing built up by the maritime Powers, England and Holland, with their flourishing national banks and mercantile companies.

The financial contrast was also an economic and social one. In England, the release of national energies under a government of very restricted claims, and of limited powers, was productive of an economic growth which owed far less to the State, than did that of France, where the system of Colbert, the local variant of mercantilism, was not simply a system of controls but also one whereby the State took an active part in industrial enterprise, initiating and developing projects for which private capital was not forthcoming. Yet by comparison with Prussia, for instance, the share of the State in the general development of eighteenth-century France seems rather a negative one. It is society rather than the State, the unofficial rather than the official world that are the truly creative elements. The names that brought lustre to France between the death of Louis XIV and the outbreak of the Revolution include those of neither of its monarchs, and of scarcely a statesman outside the field of foreign affairs.

CHAPTER IV

SPAIN AND PORTUGAL

SPAIN

The history of government in Spain between the middle of the seventeenth century and the Napoleonic conquest—the form in which Spain received the French Revolution—is divided into three periods by the accidents of dynastic succession. The first consists of the reign of the last Habsburg monarch, Charles II, 1665–1700. His long-awaited death without a direct heir had been prepared for in a series of negotiations between the European Powers who were concerned to prevent the wealth, power and prestige of the Spanish Empire in Europe and overseas from being added as a whole either to the dominions of the French monarchy, or to those of the Austrian Habsburgs, which would enable the latter to recreate the sixteenth-century Empire of Charles V. These schemes broke down owing to the ambitions of Louis XIV, and the unwillingness of the Spaniards themselves to see their Empire diminished. The War of the Spanish Succession and the treaties with which it ended confirmed, as has been seen, the principle of partition, but left the Bourbon claimant, Philip V (1700–24 and 1724–46) in undisputed possession of Spain and her overseas Empire. The second period consists of the reigns of the first three Bourbons, Philip V, Luis I (1724) and Ferdinand VI (1746–58). In the course of these reigns, an attempt was made to introduce into Spain the administrative system of the more highly-centralized monarchy of France. There was a recovery in the country's international standing and the economic decline of the past century was at least arrested. With the accession of Ferdinand's half-brother, Charles III (1758–88) a third period was inaugurated. Charles who had ruled successively as Duke of Parma, and, since 1734, as King of Naples and Sicily, was influenced if only to a limited extent, by the ideas of the enlightened despotism current in the Italian peninsula. In the first part of his reign a number of Italians held high office, and latterly a number of exceptionally able and devoted Spaniards. With their help, the process of reforming Spanish government was pushed forward and not without some result. But the graver maladies from which the Spanish monarchy suffered were not to be remedied by mere administrative improvements or by the marked progress in the country's economy. War revealed the hollowness of the financial structure. The disastrous reign of Charles IV culminating in his abdication in 1808 was sufficient proof that something more fundamental was needed. It was not provided.

A major interest of Bourbon rule in eighteenth-century Spain is thus to be found in the attempt to apply on foreign soil some of the principles of centralized government to which the French monarchy and its servants had given such prestige under Louis XIV. In a formal sense, the attempt was not unsuccessful: Spain presented the appearance of an absolute monarchy, but the overall failure of its reformers suggested that the absolutism was more apparent than real, that the condition of its existence in theory was to refrain from exercising it in practice. It would hardly suffice to explain the failure in personal terms; although none of the Bourbon monarchs of Spain, not even Charles III was personally outstanding. Two foreigners Alberoni and Ripperda held power under Philip V; the latter was little more than an adventurer, and most of their native successors, apart from Patiño, Campillo and Ensenada completely mediocre. The ministers of Charles III, the great noble Aranda, the typical bureaucrat of the new school Floridablanca, and its principal theoretician Campomanes, would all stand comparison with any of their contemporaries abroad.

The weakness of Spain was not made fully apparent until the failure of its attempt to meet the Napoleonic challenge under the rule of the Court favourite Manuel Godoy, the Prince of the Peace and the consequent abdication of Charles IV and his heir Ferdinand VII in 1808. Of this Spain, the true Spain of the decadence, Goya has left an imperishable portrait. But the failure of the dynasty was inherent in the situation which existed when Charles IV came to the throne in 1788.

Obstacles to success had been numerous. For almost a

century before the change of dynasty, Spain had been in the grip of an economic decline; a falling population; chronic unemployment and land falling out of use. The power of the Crown had decreased; the great estates, the *latifundia* had grown in size and number as had the wealth of the Church. Financial disorder had shown itself in the chaos of the currency leading to alternating bouts of inflation and deflation and to irregular price movements. These were generally downwards in the latter half of the seventeenth century with the usual depressing effect upon business. The long drain of the wars—civil as well as foreign—culminated in the loss of the Netherlands and the rest of the Burgundian inheritance as well as of Spain's Italian possessions. The social order and intellectual circumstances reflected this sorry story of Spain's decadence. The nobility, both the Court nobility of the historic grandee families and that section of it of relatively recent creation, and the country gentry, the latter reckoned in 1787 as 500,000 in numbers, one in twenty of the population, were even more securely entrenched in their privileges than that of France. Their contempt for productive occupations was even more marked; and this despite the almost proverbial poverty of a large part of the country element.

The Spanish middle-class still more hemmed in by monopolies, particularly where the Indies trade was concerned, was much weaker than that of France. In 1717, the *Casa de Contratacion*, The India House, was moved from Seville to the better port of Cadiz which had shared the American trade in a secondary capacity. From 1764 onwards in particular steps were taken to limit the monopoly of Cadiz over the American trade, and by the death of Charles III, the trade was open to all Spanish subjects and to all Spanish ports. Finally the *Casa de Contratacion* through which the trade had been regulated for 287 years was abolished in 1790. But the new liberalization of the outwardly formidable if often defied apparatus of Spanish mercantilism came too late to have much effect upon Spanish life, and too late to save the Spanish Empire on the American mainland.

One result of middle-class backwardness was that the sale of offices was a less important feature of the financial, adminis-

trative and social system in Spain than in France. The practice
itself went back to pre-Habsburg days and by the sixteenth
century offices were regarded as freeholds. Philip II and his
successors endeavoured without success to check the practice
which their financial needs made inescapable. But the middle-
class was too poor to provide many purchasers. Furthermore,
since it was easier to be ennobled in Spain than in France and
since more people were nobles by inheritance, offices were not
sought for the titles they conferred. The higher administrative
positions, places at Court, judgeships and army commissions
were not saleable. On the other hand, the sale of municipal
offices, a late development in France had been early established
in Spain. Although these facts would seem to suggest greater
control by the monarchy over the administration than was
true of France, the resistance to change was very strong indeed.
Whether this resistance reflected primarily the rigidity of the
social structure, or certain aspects of the national character and
religion, or whether indeed it simply arose out of the administrative system itself, with its multiplicity of commissions and
committees at every level, the whole designed for deliberation
rather than action, cannot easily be determined.

On the intellectual side, the penetration of the ideas of
the enlightenment was met with more resistance than in most
other European countries. In part, perhaps, it was due to the
fact that the *salons* of Madrid were less successful than those of
Paris in forming a focus for cultural diffusion: in part the xenophobia of the Spaniards made the new ideas the more suspect
because they were foreign. The principal factor was, no doubt,
the continued predominance of the Church. It was not for
nothing that modern Spain was the creation of a series of crusades; that Islam, Judaism and Protestantism had succumbed in
turn to extirpation, expulsions or forced conversion. With the
final banishment of the Moriscos at the beginning of the seventeenth century, its triumph had been complete. The only threat
to the absolute authority of the Church came from the monarchy
itself, and the advent of the new dynasty was almost bound to
mean some attempt to bring it into a relationship with the Crown
closer to that existing in France. Philip V secured a new con-
cordat with the Pope in 1753 which was distinctly favourable to

the Crown. In 1767, the Jesuits were expelled. Finally the Inquisition itself was subjected to some restraint and the burning of heretics already rare finally put an end to. These measures, it must be emphasized were a revolution from above; they were not popular despite some penetration of Jansenist, masonic and other influences of the Enlightenment, and the Spanish people as a whole would seemingly have been inclined to see them reversed. The Church remained powerful and wealthy. In 1787, the clergy accounted for some 200,000 of the country's population: Sixty-two thousand of these were monks and nearly thirty-three thousand, nuns. The reign of Charles IV saw a reaction towards clerical obscurantism which the monarch did nothing to discourage. As subsequent history was to show the Spanish church was far more closely integrated with Spanish society than the French church with French society. Meanwhile it contributed to giving to Spain its outstanding quality of resistance to change in any field.

Above all, though Spanish national unity could still be aroused by a foreign conqueror, particularly one suspect of godlessness, in ordinary times it was much less potent a force than local particularism, which was fortified by geography and by the appalling lack of internal communications. The domination of Castille, established at the time of the country's reconquest from the Moors, and enhanced by its monopoly of access to the overseas Empire was never willingly accepted. In many respects it was the domination of a backward pastoral economy over parts of Spain with a more varied and richer life. Southern Spain which had depended on irrigation had perhaps had the heart taken out of it with the expulsion of the Moriscos. But Catalonia with its Mediterranean outlook and Provençal culture remained in a state of permanent dissidence. The middle of the seventeenth century witnessed one great abortive rebellion, and in the War of the Spanish Succession it was in Catalonia that the strength of the defeated Habsburg claimant had lain. His defeat was Catalonia's, though not Catalonia's last. In the north-east, the Basques and Navarrese retained traditions and an outlook of their own.

In Spain, as in other European countries, both particularist and feudal opposition to the Crown had found expression in representative institutions, and the latter had consequently been allowed to decay as soon as the monarchs became strong enough to dispense with their support. In the sixteenth and seventeenth centuries six of the original twenty-two Spanish kingdoms now united under the Habsburgs still retained their own *Cortes*: Castille, Aragon, Catalonia, Valencia, Majorca and Navarre. In these assemblies of Estates, the nobles, the clergy and the towns were all represented. They had the duty of formally acknowledging the heir to the throne; and in the absence of any Spanish coronation ceremony, they took the oath of fidelity to the new monarch on his accession. In the past, they had had the power of voting on the demands for money made to them by the Crown. But in 1624, Philip II had levied taxes without them, and the *Cortes* had definitely passed into the background before the change of dynasty took place. Since the Crown was under no obligation to summon them regularly, and since they had no initiative in legislation, their position henceforward lacked any real sanction, at least under normal circumstances with an undisputed and assured succession.

Philip V was faced with the necessity of securing popular support for his claims and in May 1701 summoned a general assembly of nobles, prelates and urban representatives from all the Spanish kingdoms: but this did not rank as a *Cortes* since the unity between Philip's realms was still purely dynastic. In 1702, the *Cortes* of Aragon and Catalonia met and voted supplies: but the subsequent adherence of these provinces to the archduke Charles was used by Philip as an excuse for the final dissolution of their separate institutions. Thereafter, Castille and Aragon including Catalonia were treated as a single kingdom.

In 1709, a joint *Cortes* was held to recognize Philip's infant son Luis as the heir. In November 1712, the *Cortes* called upon Philip to renounce his rights in France, and in 1714 for a modified form of the Salic law (barring female succession) to govern the descent of the Crown in future. In 1724, a *Cortes* was held when Philip returned to the throne after the death of Luis in whose favour he had abdicated a few months earlier. In 1760, the *Cortes* met to acknowledge as heir to Charles III, the future Charles IV. In 1789, at that monarch's behest, the Salic law was secretly repealed, an action which was the origin of the nineteenth-century division of the dynasty into two rival branches. Since the *Cortes* met only eight times in the whole of the eighteenth century it cannot be considered as having had a permanent place in the structure of government. The little kingdom of Navarre retained the traditions of an earlier age by keeping its own *Cortes* which met eleven times between 1701 and 1801: but this was of no real political significance.

Indeed constitutional checks of any kind were singularly absent from the Spanish eighteenth-century scene. What struck the French observer, to judge from the memorialist Saint-Simon who was Ambassador to Philip V in 1721-2 was the ability of the monarch to have his own way when he so desired. For normal purposes, however, the royal power was institutionalized. This was not done through individual ministers as was the case in France; for although a number of individual ministries corresponding to the French Secretaries of State and Controller-General were ultimately set up, Philip V's attempt to impose the French system was largely unsuccessful. What persisted instead was the Habsburg system. And the pattern of Habsburg rule in Spain, as in Austria, was one of conciliar government. The administration consisted of a number of Councils which did their work through hearing and commenting upon written documents, a procedure whose cumbersome nature was proverbial.

Of this hierarchy of Councils, the Council of Castille which in 1707 absorbed the Council of Aragon was the real heart. Saint-Simon pointed that this single institution exercised the authority that in France was shared between the Parlements, and the whole series of political, judicial and administrative councils through which the powers of the French monarchy were exercised. "It is there," he writes, "that all public and private questions are taken in the last resort, that grants of titles are registered, that edicts and declarations are published as well as treaties of peace, gifts and pardons. In brief, it is there that all matters of public concern are transacted and that all litigation is terminated. Everything is reported to it, but nothing is argued before it; with all this power, the Council does nothing but give judgement." From the point of view of a Frenchman then, this concentration of political administrative and judicial power in a single institution working with all the formality of a court of law in the Roman tradition has an antiquated air. If one regards the development of modern administrative techniques as involving the development of distinctions between the administrative and the judicial spheres, and as substituting for deliberative bodies a clear-cut chain of command within an official hierarchy of individuals for collective responsibility, eighteenth-century Spain gives the impression of relative backwardness.

Nevertheless there were elements within the system which gave a distinct ring of modernity. Thus because the system worked so largely on the basis of written reports, the function of *rapporteur* was a highly important one and the Council made it its business to see that the corps of *rapporteurs* was recruited in a satisfactory fashion. One could not become a qualified *rapporteur* by purchase. On the contrary, aspirants were obliged to pass a competitive practical examination which took the form of drawing up a report upon a particular dossier for the preparation of which twenty-four hours was allowed.

The single undivided Council performing legislative, administrative and judicial functions was not characteristic only of the government of metropolitan Spain; the Council of the Indies whose history went back to the early years of Habsburg rule in Spain was an institution of exactly the same kind as the Council of Castille, and the parallel between the two administrations continued down the scale. The same ideal of uniformity infused the policy of the Spanish crown in Spain and in America and their legislation was as identical as the differences of climate and race permitted. When to the ordinary faults of Spanish administration was added the immense distances that separated the source of authority at Madrid from the overseas colonies the irritation of the creoles or native-born Spanish upper-class is not difficult to understand, quite apart from the rigidly mercantilist notions which governed the policies so administered, and which were only partially relaxed under Charles III.

Of the other Councils which governed affairs at home, the most important in the eighteenth century were the Council of War, reorganized by Philip V in 1706 and 1743 and again by

Charles III in 1773, and the Council of Finance. It is not surprising in view of the extreme financial embarrassment of the Spanish monarchy which was almost continuous from the beginnings of the Habsburg period that the latter body underwent even more frequent reorganization. The temptation to attempt to improve efficiency by administrative changes rather than by recasting the fiscal system, a much more difficult task, was always present. The Council of Finance and its dependent bodies underwent no fewer than ten major recastings between 1691 and 1761, after which it remained relatively unchanged in form until 1803. The Council of the Inquisition was from the formal point of view, second only to the Council of Castille. By the reign of Charles III, however, it had lost almost all its political power, though it could still deal harshly enough with individuals for even the most radical of would-be reformers to avoid attacking it directly.

The complications and delays of this system and of the provincial courts were responsible for the inordinate growth of the legal profession and of other agents concerned with seeing to the affairs of private suitors. Their task was made the more complicated and their existence the more necessary by the chaotic state of Spanish law which had of course undergone successive accretions since Roman times and was now composed of an uncharted mass of legislative edicts, compilations of customs and codes. Philip II had collected previous royal legislation into a single code in 1565, and Charles III followed his example; but the work was ill-done and came in for severe criticism. Navarre had a corpus of law no less complex. The Basque provinces had their general laws and municipal privileges. Catalonia, Aragon, Valencia and the Balearic islands, although politically absorbed by Castille, retained their separate systems of private law enshrined in numerous codes. Finally there was the separate legislation for the Indies.

It must be remembered also that in Spain (as elsewhere at this time), the important social groups were legally recognized, their members consequently enjoying special privileges. There was in Spain not merely the distinction between noble and commoner, but also the special laws applicable to the clergy and to the military, and a wide variety of separate jurisdictions for members of different branches of the royal or government service.

By a curious paradox, Spain which at the centre, relied so heavily on rule by committees and boards and whose municipal government was regulated in a similarly antiquated fashion, was where provincial and district administration were concerned a country of individual officials, the captain-generals, intendants and *corregidors* all endowed with remarkable concentrations of authority. At these levels government was at least partially effective despite the extraordinary variety, complexity and indeed confusion of its local geographical divisions. Neither the areas of local government, nor those subjected to the authority of particular tribunals, nor the dioceses, were of regular size or shape, nor even of comparable magnitude. The administrative map was a single vast palimpsest on which could be traced the deposit left by the varied history of past centuries. It was an inevitable target for all who desired to see reform.

In the provinces the Captain-Generals retained their military authority in the eighteenth century and through their presidency of the main provincial courts, the Audiences, a general supervision of the administration. But as in France, the intendants were responsible for the main burden of government work. Originally intendants were officials concerned with the details of military administration. Philip V created provincial intendants in 1718; but this measure was cancelled shortly afterwards. The office was revived permanently by Ferdinand VI in 1749. The two classes of intendant later came to be to some extent assimilated to each other. The provincial intendants had judicial powers in their provincial capitals and the surrounding districts. Charles III formally relieved them of these in 1766 in order to free them for their administrative, financial and military duties; but the Spanish tradition of confounding the judicial and administrative functions appears to have been too strong for him, and it is doubtful if his edict was fully carried into effect.

The *corregidors* had, in the districts into which the provinces were divided, an even greater sphere of action than the provincial intendants, and to enumerate their duties would be to list all the functions of government at the local level. Economic and police duties went alongside administrative, military and judicial ones —the last being exercised by deputy where the holder of the office was not a lawyer, as was the case only in certain towns. Generally feared and popularly suspected of greed and venality, the *corregidor* represented for the masses of the Spanish people the real embodiment of the power of the State.

The power of the royal administration had increased alongside the decline of the self-governing municipalities which had played so great a part in medieval Spain. The Spanish Crown had carried on in most of its dominions, a long and successful campaign to diminish their powers by subdividing the great municipalities into a multitude of smaller communes, and by rendering municipal office hereditary instead of elective. Where election survived as in the Basque provinces, the mode of election varied from place to place. Indeed the varieties of municipal government provide yet another example of the complexities of the administrative arrangements of the *ancien régime* in Spain. It would have been natural to expect the reforming zeal of Charles III and his advisers to find an outlet in reforming and simplifying the structure of municipal government; but to do so it would have been necessary to buy out the rights of existing office-holders and the transaction was outside the range of financial possibility, just as the idea of removing them without reimbursement was outside the mental horizons of the period.

Charles III did attempt, as indeed Ferdinand VI had done before him, to exercise some control over municipal finance, through the intendants, the provincial revenue officers, and ultimately the Council of Castille. But this control merely multiplied the numbers of officials and obstructed local initiative in public works. As later developments made clear, the ultimate result was likely to be the swallowing up of all unused municipal revenues in the bottomless abyss of State finance. Meanwhile the municipalities continued not only to deal with police and hygiene but also to enforce their extremely close control over such things as the supply of foodstuffs and local retail prices.

Spain, it must be noted, had no tradition of *laissez-faire*.

The central government had maintained a close control over the grain trade ever since the later Middle Ages. It is doubtful whether it had ever been effective in keeping down prices, and the new free-trade doctrines led to the abandonment of the maximum prices system in 1765. Other controls then repealed were later reimposed. Welfare services and the relief of distress, previously a matter for the Church or for private almsgiving, became in the latter part of the eighteenth century a matter of growing concern to the State. And lay organizations were formed for such purposes in the main cities with strong support from the Government. An attempt to compel the beggar and vagabond to work in return for sustenance, to introduce that is to say something like a workhouse system met as usual with popular resistance, and was regarded as a piece of police oppression on a par with the naval press-gang, and military conscription.

Strength rather than welfare was the real principal objective of the absolutist monarch; and Spain a country created largely by the sword had long been pre-eminent on the battlefield. The latter part of Thirty Years War had seen the end of this pre-eminence and Spain's decline in this respect had been a commonplace. To some extent, no doubt, this had been due to the lack of military interests on the part of all the eighteenth-century Spanish kings after Philip V; and even his original enthusiasm had waned after the successful conclusion of the war over the succession. Even so there were a series of wars throughout his reign culminating in the exhausting War of the Austrian Succession. In the circumstances the economic recovery of the reign and the half-century of stability in prices and in the currency in which it was reflected, though undoubtedly facilitated by world conditions, makes it difficult to pass too harsh a judgement on the administrators of the period. The people at large seem, however, to have reflected their rulers' indifference. The educated classes preferred the Church, the judiciary or the civil administration to a military career and the development of the military art stagnated accordingly. The rule that two-thirds of all commissions should be reserved for cadets of the military colleges could not be made effective, nor was it possible to enforce in most regiments the old rule that cadets should be of

noble birth. There was seemingly nothing which corresponded
to the pressure from the French nobility to reserve the military
career for their own class and in the latter part of the century
more than half the Spanish officers were commoners. Under
Ferdinand VI, the last eleven years of whose reign were passed
at peace, and again under Charles III various reforms in administration were undertaken but the paper strength put in 1775 at
130,000 men was believed vastly to overestimate forces which
though including many foreigners may not in fact have totalled
more than 50,000. In 1803, Godoy made a final effort to remodel
the army on French lines but had neither the strength nor the
perseverance to impose his reforms on a nation obstructive to all
change.

Despite the poverty of most Spaniards there was nothing to
attract them to the brutal life of the private soldier of that
period and even the thin ranks of the army could not be maintained by volunteer recruitment. It was virtually confined to the
surviving foreign regiments which had now lost much of their
former renown, and to the household troops. Charles III tried
to organize a system of conscription with a ballot to decide who
should actually be enrolled. But the system was largely vitiated
by the wholesale exemptions which could not be avoided in a
country so constituted as eighteenth-century Spain, and it fell
with undue heaviness upon the poorest classes in society. The
privileged provinces struggled against the system with great
vehemence, and in Catalonia and the Basque country with
success. Even in Castille, the law was applied with great cir-
cumspection and produced only a small number of recruits.
These were supposed to serve for eight years, but after the first
year were released for an annual period of four months in
order to assist with the harvest. The numbers were made up by
occasionally rounding up in the great cities the vagabonds and
other undesirable elements whose presence in the army no
doubt contributed to its notoriously high desertion-rate.

The most distinguished corps was the artillery, and the
Spanish arsenals produced material of good quality although
improvements introduced in the latter part of the century were
primarily the result of the belated copying of French models.
Outside the regular army proper, the Spanish Crown could call

on the local forces of Navarre and the Basque provinces. These gave a good account of themselves in the French War of 1792-5. In Castille a considerable proportion of the population was organized into a militia or reserve force whose members received some desirable legal and fiscal privileges. But all this did not amount to Spain's being a Great Power on land; and Godoy's efforts to temporize with Napoleon can be defended as an inevitable product of the country's real weakness.

Spain at sea was a different matter from Spain on land; there were no maritime Pyrenees, and the Empire could not have survived without some measure of naval strength. In fact, this strength had largely disappeared by the end of the seventeenth century, and it was only after Philip V was securely on the throne that he turned to the task of reviving the ancient maritime power of his new country. Under Alberoni there took place what has been described as the renaissance of the Spanish navy. But the disastrous failure of the expedition against Sicily in 1718 destroyed almost the whole fruits of this first effort. Others followed, and by the time of the war against Great Britain in the 1740s, Spain's prowess at sea was once more something to be reckoned with. The problem was one of manpower more than of ship-building for which Spain was well-equipped; and measures for drawing up a seamen's register were set on foot in 1726. In 1737, it came into force despite strong local objections. In peacetime the system worked well enough, but to man the fleet in wartime was only possible by virtue of the harshest measures. The press-gang was by no means a purely British institution.

In the 1750s the fleet once more declined and the Seven Years War saw considerable losses. But a renewed effort followed, and though the navy again suffered severely in the course of Spanish intervention in the War of American Independence, it was not without its successes. In the latter part of Charles III's reign, progress was resumed and a considerable fleet was set on foot in the war against French revolutionaries while Spanish privateers were also active. On the other hand, the country was now building ships at a faster rate than crews and equipment could be provided in a country lacking in both sailors and money. This disproportion between the size of the

What is the 'press gang'?

Spanish fleet and its effectiveness is the background to the catastrophic losses suffered in the war against England at France's side from 1796 to 1802 and then at Trafalgar. Sea-power is not a thing which can be improvised; it makes heavy and continuous demands upon a country's administration and finance.

In administration, one has the feeling that one of the main weaknesses was that Spanish government, central as well as local, endeavoured to do too much; that its ambitions were altogether out of scale with its means. Where finance was concerned the picture is a simpler one. Spain was not a poor country by contemporary standards; but its wealth could not easily be tapped for the purposes of the State. Even in Spain's golden age, her government's record in finance was punctuated with bankruptcies. Spain in decline could expect no better.

The inquiries into the national wealth which were made on a fairly considerable scale in 1763, 1787 and 1797 can hardly be looked to for statistical information, according to modern standards of accuracy, but there can be no mistaking the impression they leave of enormous inequalities in the distribution of property and income. In the latter half of the century real wages declined as in other western countries. To those who cherish the illusion that inequality of fortunes is a product of the industrial revolution, eighteenth-century Spain, a country relatively little touched by industrial development even in the reign of Charles III, provides a convincing refutation. In particular was it true that a great part of the agricultural population, the overwhelming part in a province like Seville, consisted of landless day-labourers rather than peasants; and their lot was harsh indeed. Agricultural reform in the latter part of the century probably swelled the numbers of the urban proletariat.

In such a social system the task of the tax-collector is apt to be a difficult one. The taxes appeared to be not particularly heavy but their burden was everywhere felt as excessive. It was not that the system was based on inequitable principles; the nobles and clergy were not exempt and indirect taxation was levied for preference on articles of luxury rather than neces-sities. The nobility avoided important transfer dues by entailing their estates. The use of State monopolies to increase revenue was so universal in Europe as to call for no special comment except from a British historian for whom they represent a much earlier stage in financial history.

Since direct taxation was difficult to levy, as it always is in a largely agricultural economy, indirect taxation of various kinds was the main standby of the State. As successive monarchs had found their resources insufficient they had tried to remedy the situation by adding to the number of taxes rather than by raising their levels. As a result the fiscal system was exceedingly complicated and vexatious, acting as a real break upon internal economic development. It is not to be imagined that the Spanish kings or their servants were unaware of the deficiencies of the fiscal system. In the reign of Ferdinand VI, it was suggested that all internal taxes might be replaced by a single grain-tax levied at the mills. Enseñada, like Patiño a bourgeois by origin, took the matter up and obtained from Pope Benedict XIV approval for a scheme by which under such a new system of taxation, the clergy might be taxed at the same rate as the laity. A great investigation was set on foot to decide the details of the new tax and 150 volumes of statistical material were assembled. Before the inquiry was complete a royal edict of 1749 ordered that all internal taxes should be replaced by a single one on all forms of wealth; but it was not carried into effect. A similar edict for a single-tax system in Castille was issued by Charles III in 1770; but the forces of opposition were too strong and once again nothing was done. All reforms were bound to be opposed not only by those to whom the existing system gave privileges but also by the middle-class who saw in the swollen fiscal machinery an endless source of employment for their sons.

Philip V found that not only had his predecessors disposed of the greater part of the ancient Crown lands, once considerable, but had even sold in perpetuity important sources of revenue such as the products of particular taxes. To repurchase them was beyond the means of the House of Bourbon and although Charles III gave serious consideration to the idea he was forced to abandon it. Under his successor efforts were made to increase the burdens on the clergy, a considerable element in the royal budget. It is typical of the conservatism of the Spanish system that as late as 1801, the Crown was still drawing considerable sums through the sale of indulgences, first agreed to by Pope Julius II at the beginning of the sixteenth century in order to aid the alleged crusading intentions of the Spanish Crown.

The principal taxes were, however, in Castille the *alcabala* and *millones* respectively a sales tax on each transaction including those arising in the course of foreign trade, and an excise on meat, wine, vinegar, oil, soap and candles. Other commodities also paid a variety of excise dues. In 1785, Florida-Blanca sought to add to all this a sort of income-tax on rents, dues in kind, industrial produce and on royal privileges in private hands. But it proved difficult to administer and in 1794 was abandoned in favour of a new system of direct taxation with the specific object of paying off some of the State's indebtedness. The customs duties and taxes on wool were applicable not only to Castille but to the whole country except for Navarre and the Basque provinces which contrived to remain outside the Spanish customs frontier.

The customs barrier was not merely an external one; some internal barriers also survived, though reduced under Philip V: between Castille and Valencia until 1717 and on the border of Andalusia until as late as 1778, when the freeing of trade with the Indies removed its main point. In 1783, Spain acquired its first general customs tariff. This followed the assumption in 1750 by the State of direct control over the customs administration. Despite efforts by Alberoni to use the tariff weapon as a means of furthering Spain's interests, the customs which were farmed out had tended, it would seem, to favour the foreign as against the native trader. Since export duties were levied at a much higher rate than import duties there was also a marked discrimination against native industry. All this was reversed by the 1783 tariff, but the new system was so cumbersome and burdensome on the foreigner as to make the doing of business by foreign merchants almost impossible. Smuggling, long a major Spanish industry, rose to new heights of efficiency now that the profits to be made were more substantial than ever.

The principal monopolies were tobacco and salt. The latter

involved a high price for salt. But it was less burdensome than the French *gabelle* since there were no limits on total consumption as in some French provinces and no exemptions. Even the clergy paid. The Spanish government had early had the idea of a stamp tax and a government monopoly of stamped paper required for all legal transactions including the business of the ecclesiastical courts, and even the Inquisition, went back to 1636. Playing-cards was another royal monopoly as were seven important raw materials: saltpetre, sulphur, gunpowder, lead, antimony, vermilion dye and lacquer. Another source of revenue was the royal lottery introduced by Charles III for his former kingdom of Naples which in turn had imitated it from Rome.

Aragon though losing its political liberties after the war of the Spanish Succession had not been subjected to the full rigours of the Castillian financial system and avoided the *alcabala* and *millones*. Instead the Aragonese provinces paid a single lump sum which in turn was raised by direct taxation which varied in form in the different provinces but which was both lighter in total and less complicated to levy. In Catalonia, the important cloth industry was burdened with a tax upon each piece of stuff which had to be individually marked with the tax-collector's seal. Under Charles III, this was abolished in favour of a simple direct tax. Navarre and the Basque provinces retained a financial system wholly separate from that of the rest of Spain.

In financial administration, the system of rule by committee was departed from in fact though not in theory. Formal authority rested with the Royal and Supreme Council of Finance, but during the eighteenth century power came to rest with the Minister of Finance and his staff. This position was attained by degrees. The first Superintendent-General of Finance was created in 1687. In 1709, Philip V appointed the Frenchman Orry as Controller-General and director of all financial matters. In 1714, a General Intendant of the Council of Finance was created; in 1716, an Administrator-General and in 1724 a Secretary of Finance. Finally in 1726, Joseph Patiño united in his person the titles of Secretary of State and Superintendent of Finances. A struggle ensued between the Minister and the

Council; but in 1742 the Superintendent of Finances was given plenary powers over the whole field.

Below the Minister was a large organization both central and local for the levying and control of the revenues. Impressive in size and formal symmetry, it was less so in practice. This was largely due to the extreme corruption at the lower levels of the service almost inevitable in view of the poor remuneration received by its employees.

The indirect taxes of Castille were levied by tax-farmers and Orry began an effort to rationalize their proceedings and to reduce the depredations of their agents. In 1741, the minister Campillo ordered the tax-farmers to declare their profits and when these were declared at a low level removed six provinces from their jurisdiction. In 1749 Ferdinand VI extended the system of direct collection to the remaining sixteen provinces. This by no means ended all abuses. In some localities, private persons levied for their own profit a whole or part of the taxes; elsewhere there were various forms of compounding in force; the sums exacted varied in the different towns and as with the customs, interminable delays on trade were the result of an over-minute elaboration of the regulations. A system of spies and informers did not prevent fraud so much as give rise to further corruption.

The year 1692 witnessed another in the long line of Spanish royal bankruptcies. Philip V was faced with a seemingly hopeless situation. In the first year of his reign, taxation covered only some three-fifths of the country's expenditure. The Succession War and afterwards the unsuccessful Sicilian expedition and the wars brought on by the ambitions of Elizabeth Farnese were further blows to the national solvency. Nevertheless, careful administration by Orry and Patiño brought up the Crown's receipts. The fiscal recovery was, of course, assisted by the economic revival, itself encouraged by protective devices, the establishment of model factories, measures to attract foreign artisans—all suggested, no doubt, by the policies devised by Colbert for Louis XIV and now imported by Philip's French mentors, Amelot and Orry, and applied by Spaniards like Patiño, Campillo and Ensenada.

Expenditure, however, more than kept pace with growing

revenues. In 1739, it was necessary to suspend payments on the State debt in order to meet the needs of the army and in 1748 at the time of the Treaty of Aix-la-Chapelle, the financial chaos was at its worst. Ferdinand VI tried various expedients including a refusal to pay the debts of his predecessor and was assisted by the arrival, after the conclusion of peace, of the American treasure-fleets immobilized since 1742. Although much of the taxation of the Indies went to the upkeep of the local administration, the proceeds of certain taxes there and of the royal monopolies were earmarked for the Spanish home government's use. Even so and despite the interval of peace, the Spanish treasury was nearly empty at Ferdinand's death.

With the accession of Charles III a new spirit entered the administration and it is probable that from the beginning the new monarch realized that a trial of strength with Great Britain was coming and that he devoted himself to preparing for it. On the economic side he was favoured by the general price inflation which, as already noted, meant a fall in real wages and a rise in profits which meant that there was capital available for investment in the new industries which the policies of Charles and his ministers were intended to encourage. In particular something was at last done about road-building. The manufacture of cotton had begun at Barcelona as early as 1746 but it is from Charles's reign that the modern industrial history of Catalonia begins. It is probable, however, that the excitement of foreign travellers over these developments should not be taken at its face value; the social and educational backwardness of the country were still a major impediment to rapid progress.

This economic revival was sufficient to lead to a new and major advance in the royal revenues; but expenses still ran ahead of receipts and under Charles IV the rise in revenue came to an end while the deficit grew. The efforts of Charles III to increase the revenue were mainly directed against the Church. The expulsion of the Jesuits involved the confiscation of their property: the income from vacant benefices was appropriated for an indefinite duration and the possessions of pious foundations were sold for the benefit of the treasury. Further and even more desperate measures were taken by his successor, at the expense of all classes of society. Again, however, the Church was the principal sufferer. Only the fall of the dynasty at Napoleon's hands in 1808 brought the process of confiscation to a halt.

The importance of the question of ecclesiastical revenues in Spain's national finances at the turn of the eighteenth century is indicative of the relative backwardness of the economy and social and political institutions of the country. The difficulties which arose in attempting to fill, by borrowing, the remaining gap between revenue and expenditure are to be explained along the same lines. The ability to raise loans easily and on favourable terms was in many ways the principal achievement of the modern State in its formative period and the state of public credit is not a bad index to the success or failure of particular polities in the age under consideration.

Charles III raised money at home by the sale of annuities and abroad on the Dutch money-market, the latter in particular for one of his great public works the Aragon canal. A whole series of loans were issued both in his reign and his successor's. But their nominal total was not in fact reached, for despite the highly favourable terms offered, subscriptions could only be obtained by offering the loans at well below par; and even then many were not taken up in full. More important was the money procured from the existing financial institutions, the *Consulados* of Seville and Cadiz, the associations of merchants in the American trade, whose position was being weakened by the ending of their monopoly, and who were now forced in addition to come to the rescue of the treasury, and the five major Corporations or Guilds of Madrid who had in the past acquired through the careful use of their resources a standing which the State could not emulate. The exactions of Charles IV brought their financial structure down in ruins.

It was the participation of Spain in the War of American Independence that marked the beginning of the major financial troubles of the reign since it led to the issue of an interest-bearing paper currency forced on the market by legislative fiat. While the war was on the value of this currency naturally depreciated but there was a recovery after the Peace of Paris in 1783, with the renewal of shipments from America. A further blow at financial stability was struck by the war against England that broke out in 1796. It is a curious comment on the inadequacy of the Spanish financial system and on the pervasive effect of Spain's adverse trade balance that although the mines of Spanish America provided a great deal of the currency in which the international trade of the period was carried on, it proved almost impossible in the eighteenth century to provide an adequate currency for use at home or even in small denominations for the American colonies themselves. The paper currency did not circulate in the colonies though the colonists were taxed in order to redeem it and suffered from the economic effects of the dislocation at home. As was to be expected, there was a Spanish effort to do what Holland and England alone had done successfully, to establish a national bank with the express purpose of managing more economically than through merchant-syndicates the indebtedness of the State and for sustaining its credit.

As in France it had been the Scot John Law who had been the prime mover, so in Spain also it was a foreigner: in this case actually a Frenchman, François Cabarrus. His proposal for a new financial institution was put forward during the period of Spain's intervention in the American war and the Bank of St. Charles, as it was called, was founded by royal decree in 1782.

After a slow start, the Bank began to acquire prestige but it allowed itself to indulge in a series of highly speculative enterprises such as the very costly proposal to connect Madrid with the sea by canal, and an attempt to profit by the exceedingly low price of French government bonds in 1788. But it was finally the task laid upon the Bank of redeeming the floating debt of the monarchy that reduced it to the straits in which it found itself on the fall of the dynasty. The Bank of St. Charles emphasized the lesson which should have been learned from the failure of Law. The successes of the Bank of Amsterdam and of the Bank of England was due to the fact that they fulfilled the requirements of the moneyed classes of the two countries. Their credit maintained that of the State. In Spain as in France, no such external support existed and the credit of the Bank could in fact be no greater than that of the State which it served.

PORTUGAL

The history of Portugal in the century and a half between

the recovery of its independence and the French Revolution provides an obvious parallel with that of Spain, although it was the France of Louis XIV that seems to have provided the most direct inspiration for Portuguese absolutism and its policies. The revolt of Portugal from its sixty years of subjection to Spain had taken place in 1640, but its sovereignty under the native house of Braganza was not recognized by the Spaniards until 1668 and then largely as a result of the existing international situation, it being the price Spain paid for ending the close association of Portugal with France.

Portugal was indeed incapable of an isolated existence or wholly autonomous development. In 1641, her ports had been opened to foreign traders and in 1654 a commercial treaty with the Cromwellian Protectorate laid the foundations of British supremacy in her economic affairs. Independence also found Portugal with a declining agriculture connected it would seem with a lack of man-power. Ericeira the dominant minister from 1675 of the regent Pedro (later King Pedro II) had introduced protectionist legislation to supplement the sumptuary laws by which his predecessors had endeavoured to remedy the unfavourable balance of trade. The model was again clearly the work of Colbert in France. But as was inevitable with a system dependent on the shifting and uncertain will of a royal house so deficient in kingly qualities as that of Braganza in this period, nothing much came of Ericeira's projects and upon his death in 1690 their development came to an end. By the Methuen Treaty of commerce with Great Britain in 1703, the nascent Portuguese woollen industry was sacrificed for the sake of the wine trade and for most of the remainder of the century, the Portuguese and Brazilian markets for English goods were an important factor in European affairs. The Portuguese market itself widened during the early years of the eighteenth century thanks to the influx of Brazilian gold. Portugal's colonial Empire had suffered during the period of the country's subjection to Spain and in the East Indies never recovered. But the Dutch effort to conquer Brazil as well was ultimately foiled by 1654 and Brazil (with the African colonies as a source of slaves) became the centre of Portugal's interests. Hopes that Brazil would be a major source of mineral wealth had been disappointed for a long time, and although some mines were known in the first half of the seventeenth century, it was only later that the richer seams were found and only in the century's last decade that a steady output was received leading in the next twenty or thirty years to a veritable gold-rush.

Portugal was no more suited than Spain to cope with the obligations and temptations of such an imperial position. The medieval *Cortes* were revived under the new dynasty and in the early years of John IV, its first monarch, they continued to approve new taxation. This function, however, fell into abeyance and under Pedro II, the *Cortes* met only three times, and then simply for the purpose of dealing with various problems of the succession. After 1697 the *Cortes* vanished altogether and from then until 1820, Portugal provided a thoroughgoing example of an hereditary, absolute monarchy.

John V (1706–50) set himself to profit by his position through a lavish use of money particularly for building purposes, that suggests the full strength of Louis XIV's example. His financial difficulties and those of his successors can hardly be set down to the account of military expenditure. After the War of the Spanish Succession, Portugal's history was relatively peaceful, and no attempt was made to keep effective forces under arms. The war against Spain in 1762–3 and against revolutionary France after 1793 fully revealed Portuguese deficiences in this respect.

The major causes of the difficulties of the Portuguese Crown, apart from royal extravagance, were indeed to be found in the disorder and corruption of the financial administration and in the fact that large portions of the Crown's nominal revenues had been mortgaged to private persons. There was a recovery after the peace with Spain in 1715. In part this was due directly to the royal revenues from Brazil some 3,000,000 out of 16,000,000 cruzados, in part to the influx thence of private wealth which sent up the taxable capacity of the country without the necessity for new taxes, thus incidentally making possible the disappearance of the *Cortes*. By 1730, a measure of financial stability was reached, and the outstanding State loans were converted at favourable rates. Nevertheless, the economic state of the country was an unhappy one and with the administrative lethargy and nepotism of the last years of John V, Portugal was generally regarded as a State in decay. Attempts to remedy matters by legislative activity such as a new compilation of protectionist laws drawn up in 1749, foundered on the lack of energetic ministers.

Energy, if nothing else, was restored to the Portuguese State in the following reign, that of Joseph I (1750–77), by the domination of a new and remarkable minister, Pombal. The latter came from the small rural nobility, a natural source of servants for absolutist monarchs, but had married his way into the Court nobility who had hitherto dominated the Portuguese State. Pombal has often been described in terms which suggest that, under his administration, Portugal underwent some of the influence of the enlightenment. In fact, however, the deep superstition of the country, upheld by the Inquisition and by censorship was not disturbed. Nor were Pombal's practical measures in tune with a Europe where the free-trading ideas of the physiocrats were already gaining ground. In spite of the fact that he seems to have been influenced to seek the causes of Portugal's weakness by his study of England during his residence in London as Ambassador from 1740 to 1744, his policy was really another attempt to adapt the methods of Colbert and the French mercantilists.

Pombal reorganized the Brazilian mines, regulated the trade in tobacco and sugar and in 1771 took over the diamond trade for the State. In 1756 a new Council of Commerce was given important powers for the regulation of foreign commerce and used them to curtail the business and privileges of the English. Efforts to restrict the export of the precious metals were less successful, since Portugal could not do without imports including imports of grain. In the struggle to develop native commerce, the lack of a strong literate middle class was a major obstacle. Neither an attempt to interest the nobility in such pursuits, nor ambitious plans for increased educational facilities could show immediate returns. The executive capacity of the State was insufficient to carry the State manufactures and State commercial concerns which multiplied under his regime. Whatever may be thought of the wisdom of Pombal's policies, his methods involved a high-handed tyranny which brought

Pombal

him the implacable resentment of some of the great families. In spite of his not unsuccessful efforts to remedy both the immediate and long-term effects of the great Lisbon earthquake of 1755, Pombal did not achieve popularity and was compelled to fight for his position which depended on the favour of a monarch who became increasingly superstitious after the Lisbon calamity, and increasingly under the influence of the Jesuits. The latter were among Pombal's bitterest enemies, mainly it would seem because of his struggle against the position which they had acquired in parts of Brazil where, as in neighbouring Paraguay, they exercised what amounted to political rule over large groups of Indians, whom they were here thought to be detaching from their Portuguese allegiance.

An assassination plot against the King, in which important noble families were implicated, enabled Pombal to act with vigour and brutality against both his secular and his clerical enemies. In 1759, the Jesuits were expelled from the country. After similar measures had been taken against the Order as enemies of the royal authority in France in 1764, and in Spain in 1767, it was Pombal who took the initiative with the other courts in suggesting a request to the Pope to suppress the order. The resistance of Pope Clement XIII was not maintained by his successor; and as has been seen, the Order was dissolved by Clement XIV in 1773. The wealth of the Jesuits in Portugal itself was not very considerable; but in Brazil the addition to the Crown's resources was an important one. Nevertheless and despite a reorganization of the financial administration in 1771, the closing years of the reign saw no relief from the financial embarrassments of the dynasty. Salaries and pensions were heavily in arrears. Even the colonies were swallowing up more than the revenues they brought it.

With the succession of the new sovereigns, Joseph's daughter Maria I and her uncle and consort Pedro III, the powerful minister fell, and a new ministry was drawn from the ranks of the great nobles. A series of economy measures did something to restore the immediate financial position but no fundamental changes were made. In 1778 a new legal code was projected; in 1779 the Academy of Sciences was founded; important geographical expeditions were set on foot. The foundation of the charitable *Casa Pia* of Lisbon in 1782, showed that the new humanitarianism of the late eighteenth century had its influence in Portugal as well as in Spain.

But the important thing was that Pombal had made no difference to the essential foundations of the Portuguese monarchy. Even if his schemes had been rightly conceived they must have foundered on the insufficiency of the means available for their execution. In 1792, the Queen collapsed into the madness which lasted until her death twenty-four years later. Meanwhile her son, John, Prince of Brazil, later John VI, ruled unhappily with the title of Prince Regent over a country as ill-equipped as any to face the diplomatic problems posed by the French Revolution for a country to whom the revolutionary ideals made no visible appeal. In 1807, the transfer of the court to Brazil helped to speed up the development of a new nation which the eighteenth-century growth of the Brazilian economy and mingling of the races were in a fair way to produce, and for which Portuguese absolutism could no longer suffice.

CHAPTER V

PRUSSIA AND AUSTRIA

AT the end of the Thirty Years War—a catastrophe from which Germany was long in recovering—it was already plain that the attempt to assert the authority of the Habsburg emperors outside their hereditary dominions had failed. The machinery of the Empire, the Diet, the Supreme Court, the Circles for administration ground meaninglessly on. The Emperor was one only among the German sovereigns, even if for a long time to come, the most powerful of them. During the next century the most significant development was the emergence of the Hohenzollerns of Brandenburg-Prussia as the rulers of another Great Power, so that henceforth Prussia was not simply one of the multitude of small states into which the German nation had been fragmented but something clearly superior to its rivals. It was during the Age of Absolutism that there emerged into view that polarization of Germany between Berlin and Vienna, incarnating to some extent the older division into Protestant and Catholic, which was to be the principal feature of German history in the nineteenth century.

The history of the Hohenzollerns thus provides a direct and indeed striking parallel to the history of the House of Savoy which from its base in Piedmont was ultimately to oust Austria from the control of northern Italy that it inherited from the Spanish Habsburgs as a result of the territorial settlements after the War of the Spanish Succession. It is probably no accident that Prussia proper, like Piedmont, was on the periphery of the area to which its rule was ultimately to give political unity. The stages in Prussia's geographical expansion have already been sketched. Its history provides the best example of what could be achieved by a succession of determined dynasts in the way of creating a viable realm out of decidedly heterogeneous materials.

The real founder of the country's greatness, Frederick

William the Great Elector (1640–88) had not been content to rely on military and diplomatic successes to increase and maintain his dominions. He had begun the essential work of creating a single administrative machine based primarily on the army supply organization, the *Kriegskommissariat*, and of subordinating to it the older provincial governments of the separate lands. The nobility and the towns were forced to confound their separate interests with those of the whole. But one should not read back into a seventeenth-century context the impersonal idea of the State of which later Prussian rulers were to make themselves the servants. Frederick William in his will attempted to divide up his lands again between the sons of his first and second marriages as though they were purely personal possessions.

The new elector, Frederick III secured the support of the Privy Council in setting aside a testamentary disposition that ran counter to dynasty's traditions, and after his assumption of the title of King in Prussia in 1701, royal decrees of 1710 and 1713 affirmed the unity of the Hohenzollern domains. But although Frederick inherited the basic institutions for a unitary State including an army and a bureaucracy in which Prussians, Brandenburgers and Pomeranians served alongside his very different subjects from the Catholic Rhenish provinces, the future distinction of Prussia could not easily be gauged from the record of his reign. He was as attracted as were the other German princes by the outward show of the French monarchy, and as blind to the evil consequences of the extravagance which this outward show portended. The creation of offices for sale was begun in his reign in order to meet the expenses entailed by Prussia's participation in the War of the Spanish Succession, and continued until the reign of Frederick II who abolished the practice except in the western provinces.

Frederick William I, who came to the throne in 1713, was not a sympathetic character and has interested historians largely because of the effect that the harshness he displayed towards his successor may have had upon the character of that more enigmatic figure. Nevertheless, it was Frederick William's reign that marked the real turning-point in Prussia's fortunes.

He did not indeed make any dramatic departure from precedent. But peace, rigid economy, the careful management of the royal domains and proper attention to the collection of taxes enabled him to double his revenues between his accession and his death in 1740. In the same period, the army was built up from 38,000 to over 80,000 men. When at the end of 1740, Frederick II by invading Silesia made a direct bid to alter the balance of power in central Europe, Prussia was already, militarily speaking, a Great Power.

From the formal point of view, the Prussian monarch was not yet absolute. Representative assemblies, *Landtage*, existed in Brandenburg, in Prussia and in other provinces; and there were survivals of similar institutions in the smaller scraps of Hohenzollern territory in southern and western Germany. In theory the *Landtage* still had powers over taxation and recruitment. In effect, however, the monarchs had succeeded in circumventing them by the incorporation of the landowning aristocracy into the machinery of the State. Upon the aristocracy depended also the army, Prussia's most fundamental institution.

In dealing with this aspect of the Prussian system we again come up against the fundamental cleavage between western Europe and Europe east of the Elbe, where serfdom was the dominant social institution and where the duties of the nobility towards the State were closely connected with their direct authority over their own serfs. The European standing armies had grown up in the fifteenth and sixteenth centuries as a weapon by which the monarchs might subdue their over-mighty subjects. But since, as the history of the Italian city-states had shown, the middle classes were willing to pay for their defence but not to fight, the standing armies had themselves become largely the preserve of the nobility as far as the officer corps was concerned.

The political significance of this fact varied according to the balance of social classes and other forces within the particular countries concerned. Where the middle class was politically weak it was content to leave the whole question to the monarchy provided that it was not interfered with in its own preferred pursuits. Where as in England and Holland the middle class had influence through its representatives on the levying of taxes this in turn gave it a handle in military matters. The English story is usually told as though the problem was solved by the end of the seventeenth century, after which the armed forces depended for their financial support upon annual appropriations and for their discipline upon an annual Mutiny Act. But the matter was much less simple since the army officers continued to form if not a class at least an important vested interest and to act accordingly. Parliamentary seats were used by officers as a means of professional advancement; sixty-four serving army officers were elected to Parliament in 1761 as well as a number of naval officers. After the Revolutionary and Napoleonic wars this came to an end and henceforth army interests were guarded by the retired officers sitting in Parliament. From 1794, too, the office of the Commander-in-Chief, the "Horse Guards" also devoted itself to defending the interests of the military against the civilian interests represented by the War Office. As far as England is concerned it was only the abolition of the purchase of commissions in 1871 that ended the *ancien régime* in the army.

If in parliamentary and pacific England the officering of the army by the landed gentry and the mechanisms by which this employment was assured were social phenomena of such significance, their importance under quasi-feudal conditions, such as existed in Prussia, is readily understandable. The nobles were able to exact rewards more important than the right to regard commissions in the army as property enjoying a market price. What they wanted was not only exemption from plebeian burdens of taxation and billeting, but above all power within their estates. In 1653, the Great Elector was granted by the Estates the right to maintain a standing army, and six years' taxes towards its upkeep, while the peasantry was finally reduced to complete serfdom. It was an implicit bargain of the kind which we shall come across again when we deal with Russia.

After 1721 a scheme was developed which gave the Prussian landowner even further privileges. If he held a captaincy, he could now bring into the army serfs belonging to himself or his relatives, and after exercising them for a few months send them back "on leave" for work on the land. As elsewhere the nobility insisted that service as officers should be a monopoly of their class. Whereas the two best generals of the Great Elector's day had been men of middle-class origin, only nobles could now attain military eminence.

These measures can only be understood in the light of the economic position of the Prussian nobility. In contrast to the nobles of southern and western Germany who lived on their rents, the poorer nobles of north-eastern Germany were themselves active in the management of their Estates. The work they did for the Crown in collecting taxes, on exercising criminal justice where the peasants were concerned, and in recruitment went alongside their economic rôle as agricultural *entrepreneurs*. Even so, however, their estates were not large enough to guarantee them an income suitable to their station, and public employment in the first place in the army was essential to the majority of them, in Brandenburg and Pomerania, as in Silesia after its incorporation into the Hohenzollern kingdom. Like other rulers in the period, the Prussian kings found it difficult to get the nobles to accept regular training as the necessary counterpart of their military privileges. It was Frederick II who developed the annual musters into what became regular autumn manœuvres. Even so, as long as the nobles held on to their monopoly, training requirements could be got round. Later in the century the demand for commissions was greater than the number available, and we find the Prussian nobles entering and claiming privileges in technical corps like the artillery and engineers that had previously been despised. Earlier there had been a development in the opposite direction; for at the end of the Seven Years' War, Prussia's losses caused a shortage of officers and it was necessary to admit some bourgeois, though the nobles took advantage of the prevailing scarcity in order to get better terms for themselves. Frederick II himself believed that only nobles could make good officers. Legislation to make noble lands inalienable was also enacted with this in mind. The noble class was thus almost closed to new entrants. On the other hand it was essential to prevent the officers developing too much of a caste spirit, and Frederick attempted to meet this danger by making much of distinctions in army rank and by employing nobles from outside his own kingdom—refugee Hungarian Protestants for instance—so that the bourgeois officers in the Prussian army were actually outnumbered by the foreigners. On the other hand the eighteenth-century decline in the landed revenues of the Rhenish nobility increased the demand for employment to such an extent that Prussia could not satisfy it, so that we find Rhenish nobles in the service of the Emperor, and even of the Czar. Eighteenth-century cosmopolitanism is largely an economic phenomenon.

The central point occupied by the army in Frederick II's scheme of things did not affect his view of the nobility only. A healthy peasantry was necessary to fill the ranks, and peasants must be safeguarded in their holdings. Production must not be allowed to suffer through the diversion of manpower, so that conscription should only apply to younger sons. It was best of all if foreigners could be got to fight one's battles; the Prussian army was wide open to the recruitment of prisoners of war, deserters or other mercenaries. Frederick, like the *philosophes* whom he professed to admire, paid lip-service to patriotism, but he did not rely on it to win battles. Discipline was the foundation of his army and of other eighteenth-century armies. Consequently they could not be allowed to scatter in the manner necessary if they were to live off the country. Everything must be provided in supplies and magazines. The social composition of eighteenth-century armies as well as the technical development of the period help explain their tactics and their strategy. The war of limited liability was, as we have seen, forced upon the dynasts by the weapons they had at their disposal. Prussia in particular, founded, maintained and aggrandized by war, continued in the eighteenth century to make heavy demands upon the resources and resourcefulness of the entire country and sometimes of others for the support of her armies.

Frederick II did not, despite his early differences with his father, and his intellectual interest in the new ideas coming from France, substantially alter the course of the Prussian monarchy. In 1750 there was still a steady surplus in the treasury and it was due neither to a more intelligent system of taxation, nor to a juster social system but simply to an efficient administration in the service of a monarch in whose person the public had wholly swallowed up the private. The Lutheran idea of monarchy by divine right which had been so important in Germany made no appeal to him. The justification of the monarchy was essentially the service which it could render to the State and through the State to the people. Frederick did not consider himself an arbitrary despot but rather, the first servant of the State, working within the bounds set by its laws, and the remodelling of the judicial system and of the legal code were carried through with this in mind. On the other hand, there was in this theory of a welfare state no trace of democratic inspiration.

Frederick had a low opinion of the masses of his subjects and regarded even the benefits he conferred upon them as voluntary gifts and not as concessions to any theory of human rights. It was the arbitrary decision of the Prince which gave to his subjects the benefit of liberty of conscience, and the advantages of education according to the respective needs of the different classes of society as he saw them. Economic policy was carried forward according to the dictates of mercantilism as taught in its German form by the writers known as cameralists; its object was thus the enrichment of the community for the ultimate benefit of the treasury, and a deliberate choice on political and social grounds of the aspects of the economy to receive encouragement. In such a system as ideally conceived each individual would have his place either in the direct service of the State or in some economic activity which conduced to its well-being. But no initiative was demanded of him, no political criticism countenanced, and no sphere was available for free collaboration between the nation and its ruler. It was, as events were to show, a system at once effective and enormously brittle. In an unchanging world and with a succession of enlightened despots, enlightened despotism in Frederick's manner might seem a welcome alternative to the feudal anarchy, as well as the only one conceivable over much of Europe.

The objectives which Frederick set himself, to increase the population of his territories, to stimulate industry and so on were not novel. Nevertheless his successes entitle him to be regarded as pre-eminent among the "enlightened despots".

And despite the cultural prestige of France, for actual methods of government it was Prussia that seemed to provide the appropriate model of government for all reforming monarchs in the second half of the eighteenth century. Frederick was conscious of his rôle as an enlightened despot and happy to be regarded as its theorist. His writings round this theme bulk considerably in its literature: *Anti-Machiavel, Mémoires pour servir à l'histoire de la Maison de Brandenbourg, Considérations sur l'Etat présent du Corps Politique de l'Europe* and the two *Testaments Politiques* of 1742 and 1768, as well as the voluminous correspondence with the *philosophes* and with his fellow-rulers.

Administration even more than policy was the key to Prussian success. An essential feature of the development of a Prussian state was the development of a national bureaucracy alongside the old purchasable offices and entirely separate from them. It was recruited through examination and subject to methodical training; both venality and private patronage were excluded.

The Prussian system was originally sharply differentiated from that of France by being based on the collective responsibility of boards or "colleges" and not on the personal authority of ministers and their subordinates. At the top the four members of the principal administrative body the *General-direktorium* (the General Directory), created in 1723, exercised a range of identical functions in the different provinces so that they were mutually interdependent. The provinces were looked after by the *Kriegs-und Domänenkammern*—the chambers for war and the royal domains—in which the principle of group solidarity was even more strongly enforced. Their work was set out in detail in a written instrument, the *règlement* from which no departure was permitted. Below the chamber again were the local authorities. The more important of these was the *Steuerrat* or local commissary who supervised from six to ten towns from both the fiscal and the administrative point of view and who controlled the local *gendarmerie* with the formal reserve power of being able to call the military to his assistance when necessary. In the rural areas, the *Landrat*, a nobleman often elected by his peers was responsible for publishing royal edicts for enforcing the conscription laws, and for police. He was also nominally responsible for seeing that the laws protecting the peasant against exploitation were observed, but was hardly likely to do so to the discomfiture of his fellow-landlords.

Throughout the system absolute uniformity was insisted upon and was enforced by central control. The object was to prevent the local influence of the nobility from distorting the government's intentions. This uniformity was not unsuited to the simple social structure of the eastern agrarian provinces, but in the Rhenish provinces with their more varied economy and freer traditions, friction between the bureaucracy and the population would seem to have been endemic.

The system demanded that there should be a continual reference upwards of even local matters, and the General Directory and its officials had the task of providing the statistics and other necessary information upon which the King himself could eventually form his decisions which alone had final validity. The apex of the governmental pyramid was thus the monarch himself, and he alone could see his country's situation as a whole. Frederick believed, not without reason, that the French system of ministers under a king like Louis XV meant a lack of co-ordination. Even the General Directory could not provide this, since some provinces and some governmental activities lay outside its scope.

Under Frederick II there was nothing comparable to either the French or the Spanish councils. Apart from an annual "review of ministers" when the King approved the budgets and discussed the affairs of the different departments with their heads, the King hardly ever saw his ministers. The ministers worked in Berlin while the King lived at Potsdam. No official, not even a minister came to Potsdam except at the King's express command. Everything was done by means of written reports, sorted by the King's five personal secretaries and dealt with by him in person. This demanded of the King an almost inhuman routine of daily toil only possible because Frederick had no family ties, maintained no court and took no holidays. When he went on progress, the secretaries had to go too. The elaborate organization for handling the royal leisure at Versailles had no Prussian parallel; and few palaces have been so inappropriately named as Sans Souci.

Although the system was a thoroughly expeditious one it had its obvious flaws. Even a king like Frederick could not really be omniscient, and since initiative was discouraged and obedience insisted upon, the ministers were forced into trying to deceive him, with the connivance often, of the royal secretaries themselves. Frederick, well aware of such tendencies, developed an ineradicable suspicion of his ministers and contrived a whole system of controls to check upon what he was officially told. His annual progresses were intended to act as such a check upon the written reports, but were ineffective for the purpose. He was afraid of connivance between the Chambers and the General Directory, but since the *règlement* was kept secret, the only possible check was an internal one. A separate official, the *fiscal* was attached to the General Directory, to each Chamber and at other points in the administrative machine, to act as royal spy, and where necessary as prosecuting attorney as well. Annual reports were demanded from the presidents of the chambers on their subordinates. Promotions, removals, and punishments were the King's alone: but again he had to depend on others for knowledge of the persons concerned.

The immediate test of the system was whether it could meet the fiscal needs of the kingdom. After the Seven Years War, Frederick asked the General Directory to provide for a large increase in revenue and finding it unable to fulfil the task, set up a new separate organization the *régie* under a French tax-farmer de Launay to collect the excise taxes throughout the country. De Launay received a salary three times that of a minister, and he and his agents were given a share in the proceeds of the tax in order to stimulate their zeal.

From the fiscal point of view the measure was a success and the budgetary needs were more than met; a surplus was left which was used for the encouragement of industry. In other respects, the old Prussian fiscal system was unaltered. The peasant paid, it was reckoned, over 40 per cent of his income to the State besides his dues to his lord. And whereas the landed nobility of East Prussia and of Silesia were taxed, those of the central provinces were not. Nevertheless, because of the success of the *régie*, the Prussian financial situation compared favourably with that of other countries. A proper annual budget for central and local expenditure was maintained, in striking contrast to France, for instance, where one year's accounts ran on into the next.

From the point of view of government the main thing was that the *régie* was not subordinate to the General Directory. It was, however, neither the first nor the last separate administration. A special ministry for commerce was set up in 1741, for conquered Silesia in 1742, and for the army in 1768. Others were established later for mining and forestry. The mint, and later the Government bank and the tobacco monopoly, were also put under officers directly responsible to the King. The process of disintegration was completed when the King began to deal separately with the members of the General Directory itself which rarely reached corporate decisions after 1770. The Foreign Office and Department of Justice had always been outside its sphere, and now the whole machinery was in fact broken up into separate ministries some on a functional and some on a territorial basis. During Frederick's lifetime the lack of a properly co-ordinated central government was made up for by the energy of the King himself, and by the vigour of the seventeen provincial chambers. Although these were primarily financial organs they were also the instruments of the King's positive policies of internal colonization and the encouragement of industry. Their internal organization was a highly complicated one, and again demanded a mass of paper work. Nevertheless, the bureaucracy which was stimulated to its exertions by the lack of any internal dividing lines to hamper the promotion of the most efficient officers, remained a relatively small and compact body numbering on the eve of the French Revolution only some 14,000. It should not be forgotten, however, that in Prussia the ecclesiastical organization also performed some governmental functions. The two Protestant Churches, Lutheran and Calvinist were governed by consistories, central and local, themselves nominated by the Crown, and responsible to the General Directory. The pastors were assisted by lay councils and responsible for the parish registers and for education.

By the time of the French Revolution, however, an important change had taken place in the Prussian governmental machine. Under Frederick William I and his predecessors the civil administration had been recruited from the middle class. Frederick II, seeking to maintain the incomes of the nobles, had opened the civil service to them as well. Many important posts both central and local were reserved for nobles and gradually they infiltrated into minor offices as well. They also found promotion easier than their bourgeois competitors. Furthermore, increasing numbers of civil posts particularly at the lower levels were reserved for ex-officers. This was the only way of rewarding war veterans, and after 1799 such posts were wholly reserved for them. This put an end to the practice of choosing the higher officials from the subordinate ranks of the bureaucracy, and paved the way for the formal nineteenth-century separation between the two strata of the civil service. At the same time the training of higher civil servants had become more rigorous. In the second half of the eighteenth century attendance at a University became normal for aspirants. There they studied cameralism, that is to say political economy rather than the law as in France. Some time had also to be spent working on the royal domains which still accounted for one-fourth of the entire kingdom. Only then could they apply to the General Directory to be admitted to the examination.

The increased share of the nobility in administration had its effects upon policy. In the provincial chambers in particular, it meant the strengthening of conservative tendencies. Efforts by Frederick to emancipate the Prussian serfs, to improve their titles to their holdings, to promote enclosures or to provide safeguards against illegal feudal exactions ran up against their insurmountable opposition though there was some improvement on Crown estates. The fact that the bureaucrats were paid in part proportionately to the revenues they collected acted as an incentive to maintain things as they were, and simply to tighten up administration. The ultimate authority in the countryside was in the hands of the *Landrat*, himself a noble who had to be chosen from candidates presented by the Estates. The most that the King could do was to insist that the *Landrat* should come from some province other than the one he was appointed to. In Prussia as in other countries the apparent absolutism of the Crown was limited by a social structure which was taken for granted and which conditioned all action, if no longer all thought.

The other German states varied in the extent to which they were open to the ideas of enlightened despotism. On the one hand were such models of progress as Brunswick after the accession of Frederick's nephew Charles William Ferdinand in 1780, Saxe-Weimar where Goethe was minister for a decade, and in the south, Baden. Saxony, after the termination in 1763 of the dynastic union with Poland, and Hanover were respectably governed by the standards of the time. The latter afforded less of interest to the observer than might have been expected from the fact that the University of Göttingen which opened its doors in 1737 rapidly rose to be the leading one in the whole of Germany. But at the other extreme was the savage oppression prevailing in the two Duchies of Mecklenburg, and the obscurantism of the ecclesiastical Electorates of the lower Rhine and of the Wittelsbach regime in the Palatinate and Bavaria. Despite the struggles of the Estates which were unique in Germany in the survival of their vitality into the second half of the eighteenth century, the situation in Württemberg was little better. Everywhere it seemed as though the caprice of the rulers, and above all the amount of extravagance to which they thought themselves entitled was decisive for the happiness of their subjects— decisive, within the limits noted, for good government or the reverse. The final illustration of what the system of petty dynasts meant was afforded by Ansbach-Baireuth whose ruler having, like the then Duke of Brunswick and the Landgrave of Hesse-Cassel, sold his subjects to England to fight in the American war, ended by selling his principality itself to Prussia for cash, and retired to England on the proceeds. If German patriotism were to become a political force there seemed little prospect of strong particularist loyalties other than that to Prussia standing in its way.

Austria

The modern history of Austria begins with the reign of Charles VI who succeeded his brother Joseph I in 1711.

Under their father Leopold I, Hungary had been reconquered from the Turks, under Joseph it became clear that there was no real prospect of the main body of the dominions of the now extinct Spanish branch of the House of Habsburg passing to Austrian rule. The question was whether a new and powerful State could be forged out of the lands now ruled by the Austrian Habsburgs. These were not merely geographically separated like the lands of the Hohenzollerns, but widely dissimilar in character. What was there in common between the Austrian lands proper, the Catholic and German alpine valleys, the kingdom of Hungary where a powerful Magyar or Magyarized aristocracy lorded it over a heterogeneous peasantry largely of Slav stock, Bohemia where since the reconquest of 1620 racial and religious discontent smouldered under German Catholic rule, and finally Lombardy and the Netherlands (Belgium) where Austrian rule overlay a tradition of provincial or municipal autonomy?

The effort of Charles VI and his successors to endow their possessions with a centralized and authoritarian form of government began with the additional weakness of an uncertain succession. It was necessary for Charles if his lands were to remain undivided to substitute a constitutional link for the purely personal one which was all that held them together. Since he was without prospect of a son this had to be achieved through his daughter, Maria Theresa. The document known as the "pragmatic sanction" of 1713 which laid down a permanent law of succession for all the Habsburg lands required the sanction of the Estates of those lands in which this medieval form of representation still lingered. In 1720, the Bohemian Diet acceded to Charles' wishes without much difficulty. Hungary had a more tenacious tradition of constitutional resistance, and whereas little survived of the indigenous Bohemian nobility after the proscriptions which followed the fatal battle of the White Mountain in 1620, the Hungarian nobility was still intact. Leopold I in 1687 had indeed got the Hungarians to abrogate their seven-century old tradition of elective monarchy in favour of male succession in the Habsburg line and also the abandonment of the formal *jus resistandi*, the right of resistance upon which a section of the nobility largely on religious grounds had rebelled against the newly reimposed rule of the Emperor. At the same time Leopold had accepted a limited measure of toleration in favour of Lutherans and Calvinists; but this had not prevented a new revolt under Francis Rakoczi which aimed at establishing a crowned aristocratic republic on the Polish model. The turn of the war against Louis XIV had strengthened the Austrians against the Hungarians and in 1711 by the peace of Szatmar, the authority of Charles VI had been accepted along with guarantees of Hungary's particular liberties and of religious toleration. The agreement of 1723 by which the Pragmatic Sanction was accepted in Hungary maintained that country's special position intact.

The obstacles to the centralizing policies of Charles VI and Maria Theresa were not merely constitutional. The religious factor continued to be of importance for the Habsburg Empire until almost the end of Maria Theresa's reign; she continued to regard all religious dissent with unconcealed hostility, even when local conditions made active persecution impossible. This fact gave a handle to its rivals. In 1735, Frederick William I of Prussia announced his intention of intervening at the Imperial Diet in favour of the surviving Protestants of Bohemia. In Hungary the Orthodox Serbs were suspected of looking with too favourable an eye on the Russian Czar.

The whole outlook of Austria underwent a profound change within the period we are dealing with as a result of Frederick II's successful challenge to the Pragmatic Sanction in its international diplomatic aspect, and the consequent loss to the Habsburgs of Silesia. The lands of the Bohemian crown had, ever since the reconquest, provided a very high proportion of the dynasty's total revenues. Hungarian loyalty at the critical time prevented the Czech lands following Silesia after the Bohemian nobility had shown the fragility of the Habsburg system by swearing allegiance to the newly elected Emperor, the Bavarian Charles VII. But the loss of Silesia itself was of great consequence. It closed to Austrian commerce the Oder and Elbe rivers and forced it to seek a new outlet which was ultimately found in Trieste, an imperial free port from 1719. The commercial unity of the lands of the Bohemian crown was severed and Bohemian industry and commerce suffered thereby, particularly in view of the long tariff war with Prussia that began in 1749. Henceforward Austrian economic policy was directed towards winning markets in eastern Europe, the Balkans and in Italy; in 1783 the first boat from Vienna reached the Black Sea. Other developments also tended to divert Austrian attention to the east. The most important of these was the resettlement of the Hungarian plain after the expulsion of the Turks, an enterprise of such magnitude that eighteenth-century Hungary has been compared to the North American frontier of settlement. It was the Magyar element which, as we have seen, gained most proportionately from this movement of population, and this, too, was bound to have political results, although the most important of these did not become apparent until the next century. The Slav element in the Empire was also increased by the annexation of Galicia in 1772, a poor but fertile province with a Polish landowning class and a Ukrainian peasantry, and by that of Bukovina in 1777.

In the light of these developments the various expedients in foreign policy which presented themselves to the active mind of Joseph II are not difficult to understand. The almost landlocked Empire should, he believed, become more commercially minded, and he founded a short-lived East India Company at Trieste which was financed by Antwerp but which proved unable to compete with the Dutch. He attempted to revive the idea of Charles VI that Belgium should recover its former eminence in trade, but this broke down because France would not support him in his efforts to have the Scheldt reopened. He now turned to a project which had been in the air before, that of getting rid of Belgium altogether by exchanging it for Bavaria. The threat to the balance of power in Germany which this rounding off of the Habsburg dominions would have meant assured an opposition too strong for Joseph to overcome. An active foreign policy could only be one of alliance with Russia at Turkey's expense as in the expensive war of 1788–91, and this meant being drawn still further into the Balkans.

In economic policy the eighteenth century saw in Austria a partial transition from mercantilist to physiocratic principles.

The subsidies and controls by which it had been sought to stimulate economic life in the early part of Maria Theresa's reign gave way under the co-regency from 1765 to greater freedom. The new outlook demanded the abolition of all internal barriers to commerce. In 1753, the Bohemian lands had been brought within a single tariff system, and in 1775 they were incorporated into an Austrian-Bohemian customs union. But not only Belgium and Lombardy, but even the Tyrol, Hungary and Trieste remained outside. This was the more important in that, as far as tariff policy went, Joseph followed the cameralist preference for the encouragement of industry through high protective tariffs, such as the almost prohibitive one of 1784. It would have been logical to bring Hungary in at least, since that country was overwhelmingly agricultural while Austria and Bohemia had important industrial resources. But this was not done. Hungary had always been in a weak position to bargain on trade matters with Vienna, since at least until the acquisition of Fiume in 1776 she had no independent outlet for her trade. Now under Joseph it was feared that the unrestricted competition of Hungarian grain and wine might prove too much for the Austrian peasants. As seen through Hungarian eyes, the Hungarian market was reserved for the Austrians while the Austrian market was only open to Hungarians if no Austrian interest was affected thereby. Even if this picture of "colonial" dependence is regarded as over-drawn in view of Hungary's privileges in the matter of taxation, it is obvious that the Habsburgs' attempt to treat their empire as a single unit from the point of view of its competitive position among the Great Powers was to some extent hampered by their feeling that the original German-speaking Austrian provinces were the true basis of their strength, and that their prosperity must be safeguarded even at the expense of their other possessions. The word federal has been used in connexion with the central institutions developed by Leopold I and his successors; but Austria was never a federation of equal units.

What stood in the way of making Austria a fully-fledged bureaucratic centralized State was not, however, national or religious heterogeneity, but the fundamental class structure reflected in law and institutions. If we leave aside Belgium and

Lombardy which Maria Theresa continued to govern separately, we have in Austria, Bohemia and Hungary three countries in which the essential social relationship was that of landlord and serf, and in which the powers of the government at the local level were almost exclusively in the hands of the landlord. The middle classes upon which the "new monarchies" of western Europe had relied to counterbalance the powers of the landed aristocracy were weak. In Hungary, indeed, there was a native bourgeoisie in a few towns; elsewhere the urban populations were entirely non-Magyar. The assemblies of Estates were thus representative, not of the people, as the Bohemians were reminded by the Imperial Government in 1791, but only of certain classes. The Hungarian Diet with its Upper House of Magnates, and Lower House representing the gentry and the towns had the best claim to be regarded as a true Parliament. But the class tie in Hungary was more important than national feeling, and it was given body by the nobility's completed exemption from all direct taxation. In addition, the unique county organization of the nobles gave them a corporate sense and the habit of joint action. The ruling-class including Slovak or Magyar speaking nobles was thus in many respects a single unit. But of the 75,000 noble families recorded in the census of 1787 many, of course, were distinguished only by their legal status from the wealthier peasantry.

By the beginning of the eighteenth century some of the organs of central government in the Austrian and Bohemian lands were already staffed by paid bureaucrats on the usual absolutist model, and the growth and spread of this bureaucracy was to be the principal index of the movement towards centralization. Furthermore, the growth of such a bureaucracy meant that the language in which it operated, namely German, increased in importance even in non-German speaking lands. The future importance of the language question was thus already latent when Joseph II began his policy of conscious Germanization through his schools policy. This in its turn awakened the national sentiments particularly of the Czechs, Poles and Magyars who were required to abandon their own language as the price of access to higher education or government preferment. Supported by the clergy who feared to see their influence over their flocks disappear, a Czech revival made itself felt even before the death of Joseph II. It did not need the French Revolution to make the nationalities question a living one in Danubian Europe.

It was because the gulf between landowner and serf was so unbridgeable that national resistance of the non-German lands was so long delayed. The manor in Bohemia, for instance, was a miniature world of its own: the lord of the manor alone was a citizen of the State; the peasants for whom he was military commander, judge and tax-collector in one had no status outside it. The lord had a right to the peasant's labour-services and from that had arisen since the sixteenth century the right to prevent him moving, to decide upon his occupation and to arrange for his marriage. The land ordinance of 1627 confirmed in the harsh terms of Roman law the sharpening of rural oppression that came about when the indigenous Czech landowners were replaced by Germans. A peasant revolt in 1680 produced even more rigid legislation. There was further legislation in 1717 and 1738 which again strengthened the position of the landlords, for while they could enforce the claims to labour services which they were granted, the Government had no administrative powers to interfere in favour of those rights acknowledged as belonging to the serfs. The State was concerned to support the authority of the landlord and the taxable capacity of the country; its influence right down to the reign of Charles VI was cast in favour of the feudal tie. Nevertheless, the enhancement of the State authority was in the long run to the serf's advantage. In 1748 and 1751 reorganizations of Bohemian local government displaced the landlord's authority by that of paid officials, and under the stimulus of new ideas, Maria Theresa issued in 1775 the first measures designed to ameliorate the peasant's lot. On the Empress's own estates she began to convert labour services into a money rental.

In Hungary the change of policy had come even earlier. At the time of the Treaty of Szatmar, the power of the manorial lord in Hungary was no less absolute than in Austria or Bohemia. It was charged that for the gentry the life of the serf had no value; both the manor court and the county court could inflict the death penalty; nor could the serf give evidence in the latter against nobles or their bailiffs. The ultimate sanction of the servile system was thus in the hands of those for whose benefit it existed. Acts of the Hungarian Parliament in 1717, 1723 and 1729 increased the power of the counties to administer the laws concerning serfdom, although the last of these did give the serfs limited powers of testifying in the courts. The dependence of the Crown on the military service owed by the Hungarian nobles was, however, demonstrated by the events of 1741, and it seemed unlikely that it could ever challenge their collective hold on the peasantry. But the effort was bound to be made. In 1756, a statute relating to labour-services, was issued for Slavonia, and the more celebrated *urbarium* (protocol), for Hungary and Croatia in 1767. The legal significance of the *urbarium* was that the peasant's labour services as laid down by law had hitherto been taken as a minimum only; now the minimum was converted into a maximum, and no changes unfavourable to the peasant could be introduced in future. Special commissioners replaced the county authorities in cases involving the *urbarium*: the peasantry was for the first time in direct contact with the State machine and began to look to Vienna for protection against its oppressors. In the case of the non-Magyars this tendency was even more marked.

The loss of Silesia so crucial in other ways also marked the beginning of Maria Theresa's administrative reforms. Her principal advisers, Haugwitz and Kaunitz believed that the disaster had come about because the monarchy, unlike Prussia, was unable to make full use of its resources. Austria, too, must have a standing army and the figure of 108,000 men was fixed upon; this would involve heavy expense. Consequently, dependence upon the provincial estates had to be avoided, and fixed revenues acquired at the sole disposal of the Crown. The basis of administration had to be shifted from a feudal one to a bureaucratic one. Between 1748 and 1763 this ambitious programme was carried through to a very large extent. In 1760 the system was given a new coping-stone in a Council of State made up of officials who had the right to discuss the affairs of the whole Habsburg Empire, and to make recommendations binding on the monarch and on the provincial administration.

At the centre of affairs separate departments were created

for all the great concerns of the State. The foreign office, reorganized under the name of State chancellery, was placed under Kaunitz in 1753: the *Hofkriegsrat* (Council of War) created by Ferdinand I in the sixteenth century was reconstituted and given authority throughout the monarchy: a *Kommerzdirektorium* modelled on that of Prussia was created as the executive agency of economic policy. A supreme court for the monarchy (excluding Hungary) was set up in 1749, it being the first time that a clear-cut distinction between the administrative and the judicial function had been made in Austria. Simultaneously, the ancient chancelleries of Austria and Bohemia were abolished, and a new organ, the *Direktorium*, created to deal with political and financial matters affecting both kingdoms. In 1762, the *Direktorium* was abolished and purely financial matters handed over to a Court Treasury, while a new Bohemian-Austrian Court Chancellery dealt with political questions including taxation. Political and financial powers were reunited under Joseph II; and his successor, Leopold II, made further changes. But these were changes within a single administrative machine; Bohemia was no longer a separate dominion.

Fiscal reform was no less important. In 1748 Haugwitz persuaded the Estates of both the Austrian and the Bohemian lands to sign agreements for extra taxation, valid for a ten year period. Between 1748 and 1760 a series of measures in Austria subjected the nobility and clergy for the first time to systematic direct taxation, and converted the taxes on the peasants from personal into income taxes, though the burden on them remained much heavier than on the privileged classes. It was discovered, too, that the Estates were holding back the surplus taxation collected in good years, and that they had a secret treasure of their own. This was put an end to in 1762 when the money which had been diverted in this way was forced out of the Estates. Henceforth they were responsible only for the repartition of the totals fixed by the Government. They were forced to advance money to Vienna while agents of the central government collected the taxes, and were responsible for any deficit. But the system still remained a cumbersome one. In 1763 a poll-tax was enacted, the population being divided into twenty-four classes and the tax being levied on families each of which was taken as having five children; larger ones paid more. This measure suggests a primitive state of economy, like the Russian, with individuals, not land or income being taken as the basis for taxation. Various forms of indirect taxation including a salt-tax were also employed and there was a royal monopoly of minerals. Tax-farmers were called upon with the usual sacrifice of net revenue.

In Bohemia further ten-year bargains known as "recesses" were made with the Estates under Maria Theresa and Joseph II, but the Crown largely relied on increasing those constituents of its revenues which were not subject to the Estates at all. Since these were mainly derived from indirect taxes they increased proportionately as the country's population grew, and with it consumption. It was as though the Habsburgs were succeeding where the first two Stuarts in England had failed more than a century earlier. It is difficult to estimate the extent to which Belgium and the Italian possessions contributed to the imperial treasury apart from the cost of their own government. But a considerable sum came from the former to meet the expenses of the Seven Years' War.

From the point of view of the machinery of credit, the Habsburg monarchy was relatively well-off. Leopold I gave his guarantee to a bank set up by the municipality of Vienna in 1703. This gradually began to advance money to the Crown and to receive its revenues in payment until the major part of them came to be handled in this fashion. It later became bank of issue, partly on the basis of deposits, which charitable foundations, for instance, were obliged to keep there, and partly on the strength of its loans to the Crown. It also gave its backing to bills issued on the credit of the Estates. When Joseph came to exercise sole rule in 1780 after his fifteen years of co-regency with his mother, the Austrian financial system, aided by the long period of peace which had elapsed, was, despite many anomalous feudal survivals, capable of mobilizing important resources; and it has even been argued that it was this fact which gave Joseph the over-confidence which was at the root of his ultimate failure.

The power of the Estates waned with the loss of their

financial importance and the changes in the central government were paralleled in the provinces. From the administrative point of view the non-Hungarian part of the monarchy was divided into ten provinces, each with its superior court and administrative board. The latter, generally known as the *gubernium*, was subordinate to the *direktorium* and its successors at Vienna. In each district or "circle" of a province the official known as the *kreishauptmann*, once a servant of the Estates, but now an official of the Crown, exercised his functions under the control of the *gubernium*. He united in himself the functions of the Prussian *landrat* with those of the Prussian local commissary, and was the agent for the increasing interference of the Crown with conditions on the landed estates. The *kreishauptmann* thus, in effect, resembled the French intendant, and exercised his functions with an anti-feudal bias. The serf could carry his quarrel with his lord before him, and was not, as in Prussia, limited to the ordinary local courts dominated by the nobility. This was possible because there was no real parallel to the dependence of the Prussian crown upon the nobility for civilian, and above all military, service. The Bohemian magnates were content to live on their great landed revenues, and did not need to serve the State which built up its own machine without them.

Maria Theresa did not follow her advisers when they wished to attempt similar measures in Hungary. The principal Crown officers were indeed kept subordinate to Vienna, and important areas in the southern frontier zone were ruled directly as the "military border". But the principal agents of Habsburg rule were the greater nobles, the magnates. They were brought by Maria Theresa more and more into the service of the monarchy and the court. By living at Vienna, intermarrying with the Austrian and Bohemian nobility, and having their children educated alongside them, the Hungarian magnates were largely transformed from territorial princes into courtiers. The extravagance of court life weakened their independence; some had to borrow money from the Crown; Hungarian estates were sold to, or conferred upon Germans. The Hungarian magnates could no longer separate their interests from those of the monarchy and came to regard the union of the Crowns as permanent. In as far as there was resistance to the process of centralization, it came from the lesser nobility, the gentry whose opposition was purely directed towards the retention of their own privileges.

In many respects the objectives of Joseph II had been defined by his predecessors. But his own contribution was a notable one, and it is not without reason that his reign has been made the test case for proving the inadequency of the ideas of enlightened despotism. It was not want of familiarity with these ideas that hampered Joseph; he was widely read in the literature of reform, had travelled extensively, and knew personally most of his great contemporaries. Above all, he was hard-working. On the other hand he was not always happy in his choice of servants, though it could be argued in his defence that, under Austrian conditions, it was unlikely that he would find enough of the right men to carry out some of his more advanced ideas.

In a sense very different from that which the French Revolution was to give to those words, Joseph's watchwords might have been liberty and equality. Both liberty and equality were devices by which the State could be strengthened. If Jews and Protestants were to be freed from persecution, and encouraged to come into Austria it might be possible to rival the economic success which toleration was believed to have brought to Prussia. If the serf could be freed and allowed to choose his occupation, industry would acquire new sources of labour. Equality meant the breaking down of the groupings and orders into which the social and legal order was divided, so that all citizens should be equally subordinate to a strengthened bureaucracy, and equally tributary to the royal treasury.

Such a policy involved the hostility of the three most powerful elements in society, the Church until recently dominant in all cultural as well as spiritual life, the nobility, and the privileged urban corporations such as were found in Belgium. It was also likely to have an unsettling effect upon those classes it was intended to benefit, and who would feel that it did not go far enough. Of this there had been ample warning in the preceding reign, for the first moves of Maria Theresa towards improving the conditions of the serfs had led to wide-spread peasant revolts which Joseph himself had been obliged to have repressed by brutal military measures.

Joseph's reform of the administration was along familiar lines. A system of recruitment by merit and of security of tenure was worked out, and constant supervision ensured. As in Prussia there was a huge development of secret agents for the purpose of spying on the bureaucracy itself. Not content with reforming the machinery of government, Joseph promulgated an enormous amount of detailed legislation and initiated far-reaching inquiries and statistical surveys upon which future policy might be based.

In the sphere of law the first part of a new civil code was promulgated in 1786, a sign of the break with the Church being that divorce was taken out if its hands. A new and enlightened penal code was promulgated in 1787, and the procedure of the criminal courts was reformed in 1788, with the effect of obliterating the distinction between the classes in the enforcement of the law. Although not all the legal reforms were lasting, the procedural changes were of permanent importance.

The attack on the Church had begun before the end of co-regency despite the piety of Maria Theresa. Ideas of toleration and hostility to clericalism—the Deism of England, the Encyclopaedism of France, the Rationalism of Germany—made their way eastwards with the Freemasons and other secret societies such as the Illuminati as their most militant exponents. At the same time the ideas of Febronius that the Catholic Church might be freed to some extent from Papal control had also made themselves felt. After 1767, the monarch's consent was necessary for the promulgation of Papal bulls; in 1773, the clergy were forbidden to correspond directly with Rome. The suppression of the Jesuits in 1773 was of great significance for Austria, and even more so for Bohemia, because of their virtual monopoly of education. It made possible Joseph's own scheme of compulsory education, his founding of *gymnasia* and his reform of the Universities, which had as its primary purpose the provision of training for civil servants.

Joseph's great Patent of Toleration of 1781 recognized the Catholic Church as the dominant one, and the one solely entitled to conduct worship publicly. But the right of worship in private was granted to Lutherans, to Calvinists and to the Greek Orthodox. The minor Protestant sects, numerous in Bohemia despite all persecution, and the Deists were excluded. The Jews who had previously already had a measure of toleration were now placed on a par with the Protestants and Orthodox. Austria under Joseph was the first State to encourage Jews to enter the productive occupations, and to obtain the normal education from which centuries of intolerance had almost universally excluded them. It was also the first State to make them liable to military service, now the badge of citizenship.

Despite a personal visit from Pope Pius VI, Joseph continued to interfere with the affairs of the Church itself, cancelling certain Papal bulls, making the bishops take oaths of obedience to him, reorganizing episcopal sees and seeing that they were given to natives of the country concerned. The attack on the Church's influence in secular matters was accompanied by a large-scale dissolution of monasteries and confiscation of their property. Since it was reckoned that the Church had held three-eighths of Austrian land in mortmain, the economic effects of this release of capital was considerable. Some of the monasteries' wealth went for other religious purposes or was used for charitable, medical or educational endowment; some was sold to industrialists at low prices, and so helped to forward the Emperor's economic policies.

Industrialists also benefited from substantial tax remissions. But the fiscal policies of Joseph were intended to go much further. In 1789 after the completion of a new cadastral survey, a new tax plan was promulgated by which all land was to be taxed on an equal basis irrespective of whether it belonged to landlord and peasant. This new law signified the triumph of the physiocratic idea, but it was also a tremendous blow to privilege and one that could not be carried through. Under Leopold II, it was at once revoked, although the serf was still better off than before Joseph's changes. Meanwhile the plethora of economic legislation under Joseph and the heavy expenditure of the State, had reduced the finances to a condition much less favourable than at the beginning of the reign and brought about great stringency of credit. The reaction of the next reign was partly a reflection of the worsened financial situation.

The changes which Joseph attempted to introduce into the fiscal system were closely linked to his direct attempt to alter the relationship between the social classes. In 1781, an edict emancipated the serfs of Austria and Bohemia. At a stroke of the pen, the serfs received freedom of movement, of marriage and of occupation. A labour ordinance in the following year was, however, designed to secure the necessary labour for the landlords. In 1785 new administrative machinery was set up in the justices of the peace which was of use to the serf in disputes with his landlord. In 1789 as part of the new taxation ordinance a move was made in the direction of commuting labour services for money services among a wide category of serfs. The result of these reforms was another period of unrest and violence; those serfs who did not benefit saw no reason why they should be excluded from consideration. Those who were to be freed from service did not wait for the new laws to come into force. Before Joseph died he was engaged in measures to force recalcitrant serfs to render labour services. After his death the reaction gathered strength and was completed by 1798. But the feudal lord never recovered his right to exact unlimited labour-services and to that extent the shift towards commutation was encouraged, as it was by the increased diversification of the monarchy's economy generally.

In Austria and Bohemia the resistance of the privileged orders to Joseph's reforms was substantial and in the case of the latter the Diet put forward to Leopold constitutional demands of some importance. But on the whole it proved possible to preserve the structure of the monarchy intact. In Hungary matters were more serious. The Magyar nobility objected to the religious measures, to the attack on class privileges to the advance of centralization, and to the introduction of conscription. In 1783 the serfs of Transylvania were emancipated. A large-scale jacquerie now broke out in Hungary, and after the Emperor had put it down, Hungarian serfdom was abolished by decree in 1785. In the winter of 1788–9, the Hungarian Estates prepared for an armed rising. With Hungary refusing support for the war against Turkey, and the ever-present threat of Prussia on the border, Joseph was forced to consider compromise. A vague promise to call a Parliament was insufficient; and in 1790 most of the administrative innovations were withdrawn. The decree on serfdom never went into effect, and under Leopold II, the Hungarians received new guarantees of their autonomy.

In Belgium resistance to Joseph's reforms came from two quarters. The clerical conservatives wished to restore the old self-government of the Netherlands through the Provincial Estates. The reformers welcomed some of Joseph's policies but wished to achieve them through constitutional advance and not through the machinery of a police-state. Joseph, in fact, ignored the wide difference between the Netherlands and his Germanic lands and followed his programme through without making any allowance for them. The Patent of Toleration in 1781 aroused much opposition, but was carried through; the local bishops were supported in their differences with the Pope; an attempt was made to convert the University of Louvain into an agent of imperial propaganda. The changes in the administration and in the judiciary aroused the hostility of the vested interests which were disturbed by them. In economic policy, the same tangle between physiocratic and protectionist ideas made itself apparent as nearer home. Free-trade between the several Provinces was introduced and corporate monopolies broken down. But external tariff policy remained protectionist and the Government intervened in the provision trades to ensure cheap supplies of food. The Estates tried to resist the changes by withholding grants and at the end of 1789 declared open revolt; an independent Republic was proclaimed in January, 1790. Leopold II more astute than his predecessor, contrived a compromise which split the rebels; and the Catholic party who continued to resist, hoping for foreign aid, were suppressed by force before the end of the year. But by now Belgium lay wide open to the French Revolution.

Leopold was thus faced during his short reign (1790–2) with saving what could be saved from the wreck of his brother's ambitious schemes. It must not be thought, however, that he repudiated the ideas of the enlightened despotism. As ruler of

Tuscany after the death of his father, the Emperor Francis in 1765, Leopold had given it what some have regarded as the best government of eighteenth-century Europe. This was made easier by the fact that the little State's relation to the Habsburg Empire and the absence of any other great power on the Italian scene had enabled it to dispense with military forces. The finances, the judiciary and commercial policy were run on the most approved lines, and something was even done for the serfs. Leopold actually toyed with the idea of a constitution (based upon that of Virginia), a project which would never have commended itself to his more autocratic brother. The difference was primarily one of political tact. It was only in the reign of Leopold's son Francis II, and under the impact of the French Revolution, that Austrian rule congealed again. The limitations on reform from above were set by the obvious difficulty of preventing it merging into revolution from below.

CHAPTER VI

RUSSIA AND POLAND

"THE Age of Absolutism" in Russia may be said to have extended from the beginning of the personal rule of Peter the Great in 1689 until the assassination of Paul I in 1801. During this period, as has already been seen, the Russian Empire became an important element in the European States system and was increasingly opened to the technological and cultural impact of the West. The latter was not as novel a feature as is sometimes assumed; for the employment of foreign specialists particularly in military matters can be traced well back into the seventeenth century, and commercial exchanges to an even earlier date. Despite the Byzantine origins of its religious creed and organization, and despite the long interlude in its development when it lay under the Tartar yoke, Russia cannot be treated as though it were a separate universe to which none of the ordinary criteria of western civilization apply. As far as the upper classes were concerned, the cultural gap which was still very great when Peter and his companions so shook the not over-fastidious English of William III's London, was all but closed at the end of the eighteenth century. In the nineteenth century the educated Russian was in the mainstream of European development.

For this reason it is essential not to over-emphasize the artificiality and superficiality of the "westernization" of Russia under Peter, or of the unsubstantial nature of Catherine II's intellectual dalliance with the *philosophes*. It has been common to treat the history of Russia after Peter as though his reforms had set up some irremediable conflict within the soul of every individual Russian, condemning Russia to all eternity to swing between the poles of attraction to and repulsion from the West. It is symbolized in the contrast between the old capital, the land-locked city of Moscow and Peter's new capital, on the Neva, St. Petersburg, a "window on to the West", the latter built we note, at a cost in lives which other countries would have considered intolerable.

No doubt there were many Russians, particularly in the nineteenth century, who did, in fact, formulate their country's problems in these terms. But by then other factors had entered into the situation, notably the general increase in the importance attached to national cultures as a result of the French Revolution and still more of the reaction against it. In the eighteenth century itself the issue was presented in rather a different fashion. Peter's essential object was no more far-fetched than that of his predecessors. Ever since the "Time of Troubles" in the early seventeenth century, the rulers of Russia had been trying to rebuild the country on foundations strong enough to resist their predatory neighbours, to recommence the ingathering of all the historic Russian lands, and to see to it that the southwards and eastwards spread of Russian colonization over the steppes of European Russia and on into Siberia was carried out in such a manner as to strengthen and not weaken the structure of the State. The last of these tasks was by no means the least important. Whereas the Western Powers were separated from their colonial problems by the breadth of the oceans, the Russians (like the Austrians to some extent) had colonies on their own doorstep. How dangerous this could be was shown (not for the first time) when the Pugachov rising in 1773–5 which began among the Russian colonists of the lower Volga was joined further to the north by the Bashkirs and other indigenous peoples who resented their exploitation in the interests of the great iron industry of the Urals.

It was no more artificial for Peter to seek to enhance the authority and power of the State by borrowing financial or governmental devices from abroad than to do so by imitation in the field of technology alone. It was only more difficult; because although Russia had the basic raw materials and could acquire or train the necessary artisans to make weapons and the soldiers and even sailors to use them, administrative talent was harder to come by at home, and aroused more resentment when recruited from abroad. More important still, even the best of the known forms of administration were only suited for particular social structures. That of Russia was both unlike that of most of the rest of Europe and highly resistant to change. What determined the tragic future of Russia was not a dichotomy in the Russian soul but a dichotomy in Russian society. The upper classes—mainly the landed aristocracy and gentry with some small middle-class elements added towards the very end of the period—were indeed "westernized" by Peter and his successors, at least to the extent necessary for them to take their share in the running of the State machine. The masses of the people, living within the framework of the village community, and bound to it by serfdom were excluded from these developments except in so far as they supplied recruits and taxpayers. Between the pyramid of privilege on the one hand, and the dark unfathomable peasantry on the other, there was no intermediate class or institution to bridge the gap, or cushion the shock of conflict when it arose.

The Orthodox Church was weakened by the seventeenth-century schism between the reforming official hierarchy and the "Old Believers" with their tenacious roots in the countryside. Dissenting sects sprang up and multiplied. The hierarchy itself was totally subordinated to the State, by Peter's abolition of the Patriarchate in 1721. Henceforward under the control of a lay official, the Procurator of the Holy Synod, it was little more than the religious department of the Government. From Peter's reign too began a steady encroachment of the State upon the management of the Church lands, and leading to their eventual secularization. In the middle of the century, the Church still owned some 900,000 serfs—the real measure of wealth in a country richer in land than in men—but in 1764, its remaining lands were taken over with the serfs, and annexed to the Crown. Russia enjoyed neither the cultural benefits of a learned clergy like that of the medieval West nor the salutary tension in political life of a genuine problem of Church and State.

The Russian merchant class was also incapable of playing a rôle comparable to that of the urban bourgeoisie in much of the rest of the Continent. Its rise to commercial importance was hampered by the hold which foreign, particularly English, merchants had acquired over the country's commerce; it was only the mercantilist measures of Catherine II, her active commercial diplomacy, and her conquest of a Black Sea outlet for Russia's trade that redressed the balance. The merchants were also hindered in their attempt to share in the industrialization of the country by repeated prohibitions against the ownership of slaves and lands by non-nobles—prohibitions which remained in effect until after the turn of the century, though devices existed for circumventing them. Urban self-government, though occasionally fostered in theory, was never an important reality in practice, so that there was for the urban bourgeoisie no training in self-government or in the exercise of political rights.

Finally, there could be no question of the bureaucracy developing into a separate and creative class. The State was not wealthy enough to reward it except by titles of nobility and by the grant of lands and serfs. There was no middle class worth the name to buy its way into office. The Czar employed the nobility in the service of the State, military and civil; the nobility lived on the product of its estates which were cultivated by serf-labour. Czar—noble—peasant; the elements were the same in the eighteenth century as in the seventeenth or the sixteenth. Only their relationship was more clearly defined, and the system a more rigid one. But the rigidity must not be over-stressed; the writing of history from central records may lead to a too ready assumption that what was true in law was true in fact; the old loose-jointed Muscovite society may still have persisted as a substratum under the apparently consolidated absolutism of Peter's successors.

The wars of the seventeenth century had been crucial for the development of the Russian State. Their main objective was to win back some of the territories acquired by Poland in the late sixteenth century, in White Russia and Little Russia (the Ukraine). A third party to the conflict were the Cossacks, free fighters who had pushed their way into the southern steppes and had lived largely on forays against Turk and Tartar. From the end of the fifteenth century, their independent organization under Polish suzerainty had been acknowledged and peasants escaping from serfdom had built up agricultural settlements among them. Although hostile to Polish domination, the Cossacks had no wish to be assimilated to the increasingly depressed condition of the Russian peasantry. A revolt broke out among them and the peasants of Little Russia in 1648; and in 1654, the Cossacks agreed to become part of the Russian Empire. This precipitated a series of Russo-Polish campaigns which ended with the cession to Russia of Smolensk in 1667, and with the Poles acknowledging Russian rule in the Ukraine east of the Dnieper, and over Kiev and its district on the west bank. Kiev was formally ceded in 1686, and the Russo-Polish frontier remained unchanged thereafter for almost a century, during which Russia's expansion was at the expense of the Swedes and Turks. The remainder of the Ukraine at the end of the seventeenth century was still divided between the Poles and the Turks.

The Ukraine's hope of retaining its liberties under Russian rule was frustrated. The Cossack state was thought of as being the supreme landowner as well as a military organization. As in Russia proper, villages were distributed as rewards for service, and ownership of the land by State became theoretical. New villages were also created by incoming proprietors. Peasant and Cossack lands were alienated to large landowners and to the monasteries, and the fiscal burdens on the remaining free proprietors forced them to alienate their lands in turn. After Peter's victory over Charles XII at Poltava in 1709, the Cossacks were punished for their adherence to the Swedes by the cancellation of the Ukraine's autonomous status. More important was the fact that land confiscated from the Cossacks was handed over to incoming Great Russian proprietors. The lands which Cossack dignitaries had held in virtue of service were assimilated in status to the absolute ownership of the newcomers. Later Government attempts to keep up the numbers of free Cossacks for military reasons broke down against the resistance of the developing autocracy of the chief officer, the Hetman and the colonels of the Cossack regiments. In 1764, the Hetmanate was abolished. In 1782 the Ukrainian nobility was incorporated in that of Russia. By now the free peasants who had still formed a third of the Ukrainian population at the death of Peter had disappeared. And in 1783, Ukrainian serfdom was finally incorporated into Russian law.

Ukrainian developments reflect at second-hand and at an accelerated pace, what had been, broadly-speaking, the course of events in Russia proper. The expansion and foreign wars of the seventeenth century forced the Czars to organize the country on increasingly military lines. By 1680, the country was divided up into military districts each with its quota of persons held to military service./For the equipment and training of the troops, it was necessary to raise greater sums through taxation, and the basis of assessment was shifted from land to hearths; that is to say to families. The State thus had the same interest as the landlord in preventing the movement of the peasants into the new areas of settlement where they might avoid both their military and their fiscal obligations. The measures taken involved the administrative grouping of taxpayers both peasant and urban, and the imposition upon such groups of collective responsibility for their assigned shares of the taxes. Russia, as was shown by fundamental code of laws of 1649, was a highly stratified class society; but in every class from noble to peasant the same duty of service to the State, and the same collective responsibility for the performance of such duties was imposed.

In the countryside the unit for taxation corresponded with the landed-estate, and the landlord was given the duty of collecting the taxes and saddled with the responsibility for their payment to the central authority. Since the landlord exercised, in addition, important functions of justice and police, and represented his peasants for certain purposes in the public courts, his position was the key to the economic and the administrative system alike. These developments had the result of merging the hitherto numerous class of free peasants with that of the serfs from whom labour services were exacted. The class of actual slaves which had existed earlier was also in Peter's reign assimilated into that of the serfs.

The legislation of the State did not define the extent of the rights of the lords to the labour of their serfs which was regulated by custom, and was confined to measures for the recovery of runaways. On the whole there was a steady deterioration in the position of the serfs; and in the eighteenth century, although no general right of sale was recognized, serfs could be sold even apart from their lands and families. Serf-owners were allowed to inflict increasingly arduous punishments. The edict of 18th February, 1762, completed the process of taking the

regulation of serfdom out of the realm of public law altogether
and making it a private institution. There was, of course, a
distinction between the privately owned serfs and those owned
by the Crown, the State-serfs. In 1797, there were about
19,500,000 privately owned serfs, and about 14,500,000 State
serfs. In contradistinction to the areas of colonization in southern
Russia, private serfdom was never extended to Siberia.

The proportion of privately owned serfs in Russia to the
general population was not as great as in some other European
countries, for instance Prussia or Denmark, but it is held
that the condition of the serfs was more onerous. No doubt
there were considerable variations in the position of the
serfs if only because of the great variations in the size of
the landed-estates; in 1777, 32 per cent of the proprietors
owned less than ten serfs, 27 per cent from ten to twenty,
25 per cent from twenty to a hundred and 16 per cent over 100
each. As in the case of the slave-owners of the American South,
in the next century, the tendency would seem to have been in
the direction of larger units. Within the village-community itself
the size of the holdings also tended towards greater variation.

These facts are relevant to the unusual rôle that serfdom
played in industrial development in eighteenth-century Russia.
As might be expected, the State supplied the driving force,
particularly under Peter. His reign was a pioneering one,
particularly in metallurgy. Its organization in the Urals varied
between direct State management by Russian functionaries like
Tatistchev or foreigners like the Saxon, Hennin, and the
encouragement of private enterprise such as that which brought
wealth and eventual nobility to the Demidov family of iron-
masters. In either case the essential point was the ascription
of peasants to perform the many ancillary tasks connected
with the provision of fuel and with transport. In the older
industrial areas of central Russia also serf-labour was largely
used in industry by entrepreneurs drawn from the nobility to
whom in Peter's reign the privilege of using serf-labour was
rigidly confined. Serfs might be allowed to work in the industrial
enterprises of someone other than their owner upon the payment of compensation to him for the loss of their services.
Some were actually owned and run by serfs who had made

money through usury and trade and who paid dues to the land-lord out of their profits. The State in its enterprises also made use of peasant-artisans accepting their products in lieu of the customary labour-services.

The industrial projects of Peter's reign did not all fructify; capital was short in Russia though some was put into industry out of profits made by foreigners trading there. It has even been held that there was an absolute decline in industrial production after his death which lasted until the new and decisive move forward in the 1760s, though recent inquiries do not support this view. The country had become a single unit from the customs' point of view in 1754 and the internal market was now an increasingly important one. The organization of industry in the latter half of the century was mainly on capitalist lines, and the competition for its control between merchants and nobles, in which the former enjoyed the patronage of the Crown, ended decisively in their favour. The prohibitions on the ownership of serfs by merchants which had been relaxed at the end of Peter's reign were indeed reimposed in the middle of the century, but by now they were relatively unimportant, since serf-labour was no longer so essential. Serfs were attached to factories but were, in fact, wage-earners so that their legal status was not significant. On the other hand, serfdom in Russia generally speaking was by no means on the decline. Catherine added 800,000 private serfs to the number through the gifts of State lands to her favourites, and another 600,000 were added under Paul. The armies which thrust back the invading French in 1812 were drawn from a society in which the basic relationship was still that between serf and serf-owner.

In such circumstances it is surprising to find that Russia remained an autocracy and that while social power went with the ownership of land, this was not true of political power. It is doubtful whether the reason for this fact is to be sought in the history of the dynasty or in that of the nobility; certainly the Russian royal house was not immune from the accidents of human mortality which were, as we have seen, so inseparable from the whole practice of monarchical absolutism.

The reign of the Czar Alexis from 1645 to 1676, though it saw a number of local risings including the formidable peasant revolt under Stenka Razin centred in the newly settled region of the lower Volga and Don, enhanced the prestige and popularity of the Romanov dynasty. The short reign of his successor, Theodore (1676–82), was followed by a period of some confusion since Alexis' two remaining sons, Ivan and Peter, were still minors. As usual in such circumstances, the great court families, particularly those linked with the royal house by marriage, tried to take advantage of the situation for their own ends. The still virulent hostility felt in some quarters against the Orthodox hierarchy for its recent reforms added to the problems of government. Eventually, the boys' sister Sophia, called in the Streltsi, the praetorian guard of the Muscovite Czars, and got a hastily summoned Sobor, or Assembly of Notables, to elect her brothers as co-Czars with herself as regent for them.

In 1689, the younger boy, Peter, with the aid of an armed coup by his own partisans, put an end to the regency and assumed personal power; though co-Czar Ivan lingered on in nominal equality with him until his death seven years later. Despite the concentration of Peter's efforts upon the modernization and westernization of the Russian State, the settlement of the succession eluded him, owing to the fatal upshot of his quarrel with his elder son, Alexis, and the death in infancy of his younger son. In 1722, Peter announced that he would decide the succession himself but died without appointing an heir. In the following period, the rôle that the Streltsi (whom Peter had destroyed) had played earlier was taken over by the Guards regiments, his own creation.

The Guard on this occasion decided in favour of Peter's widow, his second wife, Catherine, a Lithuanian peasant by origin, instead of the young Peter, Alexis' son. On the death of Catherine I in 1727, Peter II was put forward by a group among the aristocracy. When he died in 1730, another aristocratic faction attempted to keep themselves in power by forging a will in which the Czar was supposed to have left the throne to his affianced bride, a member of the great house of Dolgorouki.

The Supreme Privy Council with the support of other notables set both this claim aside and the claims of the two daughters of Peter I, in favour of Anna, daughter of Peter I's long forgotten brother Ivan V and widow of the Duke of Courland. It was at this juncture that the Russian nobles made their supreme bid to turn the country into a crowned republic on the model of Sweden or Poland by presenting Anna with a set of constitutional limitations as the price of her accession. Once she had ascended the throne, however, these constitutional provisions were easily set aside with the support of the Guards' officers who were recruited from the lesser nobility which had no liking for the pretensions of the court aristocracy.

After a reign notable for the domination of Russia by Anna's German favourites—the beginning of the large rôle of the "Baltic Barons" in later Russian history—the Empress died in 1740 leaving the throne by will to her infant grand-nephew, Ivan VI. A troubled period of regency was ended by a new coup on the part of the Guards who now brought to the throne, Elizabeth, daughter of Peter I, who was regarded as a national candidate in opposition to the Germanic influences that had waxed so strong in the previous reigns. Russian favourites now replaced German ones; and the nobility reached the apex of its influence in this period and fortified its position by the legislation of Elizabeth's ill-fated nephew and successor, Peter III.

After only six months, yet another conspiracy among the Guards overthrew Peter (who was subsequently murdered) in favour of his German wife, the Empress Catherine II. After consolidating her position which remained precarious for some years, she dominated Russia and the whole of eastern Europe for a quarter of a century, being succeeded peacefully by her son, Paul I, in 1796. The half-crazy Paul was only permitted to survive for four and a half years, when a palace plot resulted in his assassination, and in the accession of his son Alexander I. Yet despite this long succession of conspiracies and assassinations, the monarchy survived with unimpaired strength. After the failure of the oligarchical party at the time of the accession of Anna, there was indeed no serious attempt at diluting the royal power; and the institutions through which it expressed itself remained substantially those created by Peter I.

Peter's approach was dominated by fiscal considerations. In the earlier part of his reign attempts were made to increase the use of the municipal machinery for the raising of taxes. A number of new departments were created for military, police and supply purposes and were endowed with separate sources of revenue. An attempt was made to simplify local administration by dividing the country up into a number of provinces, or governorships. Again the purpose was mainly to create machinery for the raising and supplying of troops. The old central fiscal machinery at Moscow was reduced to purely local significance. But even with the multiplication of indirect taxes, recourse to state-trading and the debasement of the coinage, the financial problem remained unsolved.

A second and more fundamental bout of reforms were carried through in the years 1718–22 and were partly inspired by a desire to check the depopulation which had been shown to be going on in parts of the country, owing to the weight of the fiscal burdens imposed. The unit of assessment was now altered from the hearth to the individual; but responsibility remained collective. With the aid of the new direct taxes, the profits of the mint and the salt-tax and with the addition of the revenues of the conquered provinces, the budget was re-balanced. At the same time, the amount of trade done directly by the State was cut down in favour of encouraging private industry and commerce by the customary mercantilist devices of tariffs, subsidies and privileges with regard to taxation. But control over economic life was by no means relaxed.

Just as the fiscal and commercial policies adopted by Peter were largely copied from foreign models and bear a close resemblance to those of the German rulers and their "cameralist" advisers, so his administrative reforms of this period were based largely on foreign, in this case, Swedish models. In an effort to check the confusion caused by the over-decentralization of responsibility earlier in the reign, and as a substitute for the old Council of Magnates which had declined with the decline of the old class of magnates or "Boyars", Peter had created a new institution, the Senate, composed of a number of senior officials, and this was gradually, though with difficulty, turned into a permanent and vital part of the system, dealing with matters of policy, the preparation of laws as well as exercising appellate jurisdiction.

The overlapping system of central departments was tidied up into a number of "colleges"—nine in all—each headed by a board with a President, and working to a precise system of regulations under the general supervision of the Senate. The colleges had largely to be staffed by foreigners, and after 1722 when most of these were dispensed with, the collegiate form became more and more nominal, with real power in the hands of the Presidents.

An important new office instituted in 1722 was that of procurator-general. This official was to preside over the Senate in the Czar's absence and supervise its activities. Through his own procurators attached to the colleges, these too were brought under his control. Finally he was placed at the head of the new revenue officers in the provinces, created in 1708 and known as fiscals. The office was thus an important weapon against any form of obstruction to the royal wishes.

In local administration, Peter now abandoned the scheme of ten vast provinces created by him in 1708, and divided up the country into fifty "governments" subdivided into districts, each with an elaborate administrative machinery at least on paper. Finally, he attempted to separate justice from administration as in Sweden, by placing the local courts under the control of the central college of justice instead of the local governors. But this idea ran counter to the accepted practices of the country, and the bureaucracy retained its hold over the administration of justice at least on the local level. A new source of overlapping authority was introduced by the setting up of military districts to deal with conscription and the poll-tax, for these were quite distinct from the ordinary provincial "governments". An attempt in 1721 to develop the system of urban self-government set up in 1699 as a part of the fiscal changes was as ineffective as most of the other changes in local government. The towns were controlled by a new college added for the purpose to the central administration; and the burdens of tax-collecting and policing imposed upon them were too heavy to encourage any real spirit of independence or initiative.

In fact, most of Peter's reforms in local administration broke down very shortly after his death, and a more fundamental reorganization had to await the reign of Catherine II. Despite all the elaborate machinery thus created, Peter himself showed to the end his preference for direct compulsion through the arbitrary and unrestrained use of brutal punishments on high and low alike, and for governing through the instrumentality of individual guards officers picked out to enforce his wishes whenever and wherever necessary. After his death in 1725, a new Supreme Council was created in which the sovereign's autocratic power was in some sense institutionalized, and this rather than the Senate became the real political authority in the country. But the ruler's personal authority remained for such as chose to and could exercise it.

This system of government was imposed upon a people whose consent to it was not taken for granted. Characteristic among Peter's legacies was the Preobrajensky Prikaz, the department of political police. Dissolved by Peter II, it was revived under Anna as the Secret Chancellery. It was an essential arm of despotism.

The essential reason why Peter's reforms fell short of his models and why Catherine's "enlightened despotism" in its turn was only limited in its achievements, must again be looked for in the history of Russian society rather than of Russian government. It was not only the peasantry whose future was shaped by the pressure of the Petrine State; the same was true of the nobility whose history in this period is in many respects the clue to the whole Russian situation.

The Russian nobility composed of the descendants of the old ruling family, the House of Rurik, of members of non-Russian princely families, of the Muscovite Boyars, and of the new nobility of service created in the sixteenth century, formed a landed class of a peculiar kind. Its estates constantly subdivided in the absence of any system of primogeniture, and owning their origin by now mainly to gifts from the Czar were sources of revenue rather than of social prestige or political influence. The purpose of such revenues was to enable members of this class to serve the Crown in the military and civil sphere. As in the case of the serfs an original diversity of conditions was hardened by the Petrine legislation into a rigid system based upon the needs of the State as Peter saw them.

A beginning had been made by Czar Theodore in 1682 when he had abolished the complicated system of precedence which had been not only a source of strife among the different noble families but also a source of weakness in the imperial service. Under Peter the old obligation of nobles to appear in arms with their followers—a sort of feudal levy—was abolished in favour of a direct personal obligation to serve as an officer or civil servant—an obligation which began at fifteen and was intended to last for life. Under the strict logic of the system as Peter intended it, the rights of the landlords over their serfs thus derived solely from the services which they themselves were in turn called upon to give to the State. By the celebrated edict of 1722 all the servants of the Crown were divided into fourteen ranks on parallel civil and military ladders of promotion; and access to the higher ranks brought with it hereditary nobility. It was on paper at least a formidable combination of a caste society with the "career open to talents".

The history of Russia in the eighteenth century consists largely in the effort of the nobility to escape from their obligations while retaining and, in a large measure, extending their privileges. As the crisis at the accession of the Empress Anna showed, this class ambition was of much greater importance to most of the nobles than any political rights. Peter had endeavoured to prevent nobles retreating to their own share of their patrimonial estates by introducing in 1714 the practice of entail (though without primogeniture). In this respect, too, the nobles did their best, and on the whole successfully, to circumvent the Czar's wishes; and the law was ultimately rescinded. In 1736, universal and permanent service to the State was abolished. The period of twenty-five years was fixed as the duration of a noble's obligation to the State, and in the case of more than one son in a family, one might be altogether freed so as to look after the family's estates. The participation of Russia in the Seven Years' War brought with it a ferment of new ideas through the return of officers from foreign service—a recurrent feature of Russian history. During the brief reign of Peter III, the obligation to serve was by the edict of 1762 finally abolished except for times of grave national emergency. It was true that all sorts of effective pressures still existed to make a period of service the normal thing for members of the noble class. But the edict of 1762 did mean, at least for the lesser nobility, an exodus from the capital to the provinces, and the beginning of a genuine Russian provincial society. Under Catherine this provincial society formed the basis for the corporative organization of the provincial nobility which gave them a certain rôle though necessarily a subordinate one in the running of local affairs. By the same document as set up this organization, the so-called Charter of the Nobility of 1785, various personal economic and legal privileges of the nobility were guaranteed for the future. When this emancipation is considered in connexion with the increased burdens placed upon the serfs over the same period, the contrast between western and eastern Europe in the eighteenth century can be observed at its most dramatic. Four years after Catherine's Charter of the Nobility, the French National Assembly swept away once and for all the legal foundations of French feudalism.

Poland in the seventeenth century provided the classical example of a State whose territory (second in size to Russia alone) provided no indication of her real political weight. Much is made and rightly of the devastation to which the wars of the first half of the century exposed her, thanks largely to the ambitions of her Vasa monarchs and her constant conflicts in consequence of them with Sweden, Russia and Turkey. In the latter part of the century, too, the famous exploit of King John Sobieski in 1683 when his Polish army relieved Vienna from the besieging Turks brought no particular benefit to his own country. But the failure of Poland to recover from the effects of war must be ascribed to social and institutional weaknesses which go back to the golden age of the united kingdom of Poland and Lithuania in the sixteenth century, and even earlier.

For it was in the fifteenth century that Poland lost her hold on the Black Sea; and the decay of the trans-continental trade-route through Poland brought with it a progressive decay of urban life and a total subordination of the towns to the landed gentry. The opening up of the Vistula as the main trading artery of the country enabled an important export trade in grain, flax and forest products to be carried on with the West. The beneficiaries of this development were, however, the greater landed-proprietors who reduced the bulk of the population to more and more onerous serfdom for the supply of labour or wage-service on their demesnes. The legislation of the State, dominated by the landowning class assisted in the consolidation of serfdom.

These economic changes were paralleled in the political sphere. The Polish monarchy was unable to find any force in the country on which to lean, to balance against the over-weening power of the landed classes who were fully in control of the avenues to Church as well as secular preferment. The idea of elective kingship which had left little but vestiges in most of Europe was consolidated in Poland and in a form, that of mass-election by the whole of the gentry present—many thousands in some cases—which did not conduce to regularity in the proceedings or dispassionate wisdom in the choice. In addition, ever since 1573, the monarch had been obliged on his accession to sign a series of constitutional instruments, known as the *pacta conventa* which increasingly placed limitations even on his remaining powers and rights.

The House of Deputies of the Polish Diet was not a centralizing Parliament but rather a meeting of delegates from the local assemblies of the gentry or Dietines with whom lay most of what real authority existed, administrative, judicial and even fiscal. The conception of the Diet as simply a meeting of delegates bound by their instructions explains the *liberum veto*, the demand that all decisions should be unanimous, and the far-fetched corollary that any one member could by his negative dissolve the Diet and nullify all its proceedings. The Upper House or Senate consisted of the major dignitaries of the realm, lay and spiritual. A number of them, the Senators-Resident, were deputed to form the King's Council between the biennial ordinary Diets; though the whole Senate or an extraordinary Diet could be summoned when necessary.

The only remedy in the case of the anarchy and helplessness to which the *liberum veto* might reduce the State was the formation of a Confederation, an assembly of armed nobles with their followers who with or without the King might exercise authority and even call a Diet to get necessary measures promulgated. During the interregna between the death of one monarch and the election of his successor Confederations were the only source of authority. Their formation was possible because of the leadership of certain of the greater families. For although the fiction of the equality of the entire landed class was maintained and titles on the western model rejected, there was, in fact, a world of difference between the great landowners, the Palatines, the mere squires, and finally the landless gentry who lived as hangers-on of the Palatines. Their presence was indeed essential to the great state kept by their patrons. The history of Poland in the eighteenth century is largely one of the rivalry between the largest of these connexions, that of the Czartoryskis, the "Family" as they were known, and their rivals, the Potockis, with the other ancient families linked to them.

The Polish constitution was somewhat modified by the Statute of 1717, the outcome of the Czar's mediation between his protégé, the first King of the Saxon dynasty, Augustus the Strong, and a formidable opposing confederation. The Statute further enhanced the position of the Senators-Resident and confirmed the helplessness of the monarch in the hands of the ruling oligarchy. Something was done to reduce the fiscal powers of the Dietines and to provide permanent taxes upon which the regular army that Poland now relied on could subsist. But the size of the army as fixed, 18,000 for Poland and 6,000 for Lithuania (which was always separately administered) was too small for it to protect Poland from continuing to be what it had been in the Great Northern War, a helpless field for its neighbours' warring armies and ambitions. Confederations were prohibited for the future; a vain hope. Nothing was done to tackle the real weaknesses of the constitution until the country was touched by the ideas of the enlightened despotism in the ill-fated reign of Stanislas Augustus.

The eighteenth-century Polish kings were thus helpless prisoners of the country's political system. Not only did they depend upon the Diet for all legislation and for finance, but they had no control over the administration. The principle that officials were irremovable was maintained; and new offices or a reassignment of duties were an affair of the Diet. The Senate which incorporated the heads of the official hierarchy provided a further check on the royal will. In the provinces, the sheriffs or *starosta* originally instituted as direct royal agents emancipated themselves from this control also. It is not surprising that Augustus the Strong should have contemplated handing over portions of his unwieldy realm to its enemies in return for help in making him a real king.

Augustus was unsuccessful in that Russia, the most powerful of Poland's neighbours, was content for a time to keep it as a vassal State, rather than permit others to join in sharing the spoils. The religious discrimination against Orthodox and Protestants also gave both Russia and Prussia an excuse for intervention whenever this should prove necessary. The increasing intolerance of the Poles during this period of national decline and increasing xenophobia made excuses for such intervention easy to find.

Efforts to shake the Russian domination of the country were made but these could only be successful in the existing condition of things with foreign aid. Charles XII of Sweden failed to supplant Augustus the Strong by Stanislas Leszczynski; and after the former's death, Leszczynski, father-in-law of Louis XV, inevitably became the candidate of the French-backed national party in the Convention of 1733. But Russian backing for the Saxon claimant was sufficient to turn the scales—and the war of the Polish Succession could not affect the local situation. Under Augustus III there was more talk of reform and more intrigues by the Polish noble factions but nothing could be done while Poland's friends were further away than her oppressors. In the Seven Years' War, Polish neutrality was totally disregarded; and from 1757, Russian troops were stationed in the country permanently. Upon the death of Augustus III in 1763, the "Saxon period" came to an end. But although the new King, Stanislas Poniatowski (Stanislas Augustus) was a Pole (a connexion of the Czartoryskis), and in some ways the most talented Pole of his generation, he owed his election to none of these things, but to the simple fact that he had at an early age been admitted to the favours of the great Catherine. That the Polish throne was a suitable recompense for the discarded lover of a Russian Empress was a comment at once on the workings of the dynastic principle and on existing power-relations in eastern Europe. If this is what happened to the crowned republic, it is not surprising that absolutism had its appeal to political reformers. The subsequent reform movement culminating in the new Constitution of 1791 came too late.

CHAPTER VII

THE MARITIME POWERS AND THE AMERICAN REVOLUTION

THE penetration of the absolutist regimes of eighteenth-century Europe by the ideas of the enlightenment provides the central interest of the long period of peace on the Continent between 1763 and the outbreak of an even greater cycle of wars in 1792. Some countries stood apart from the general trend to a greater or lesser extent: Italy outside Lombardy, Piedmont, Tuscany, and Naples under Charles III; the Swiss Cantons of which the most important, Berne and Zurich like Geneva were the homes of tight urban oligarchies; and as already seen, parts of Germany. Even countries relatively remote from the main currents of opinion underwent substantial renovation: Sweden under Gustavus III from 1772–92, and Denmark after the initial impulse given by the brief domination of the German physician Struensee from 1770–2. But it should be remembered that as far as the Great Powers were concerned the results of reform were still measured in military not in welfare terms. Prussia with an army of 186,000 in 1771 (capable of being raised to 218,000 in wartime) made the running; and this on a population of 5,000,000. Austria, France and Russia, with their far greater populations, could put no more men in the field. Foreign policy was governed by notions of balance to which, where necessary, smaller or weaker Powers could be sacrificed as Poland was in the partitions. More significant for the future was an event with which these great land-powers were only indirectly connected—the American Revolution.

The American Revolution was not, of course, a revolution against any form of absolutism; it took place within another political and social constellation, the world of overseas commerce and sea-power. The difference repeatedly emphasized between the essential characteristics of eastern and western

152

Europe, is magnified when we turn to the maritime powers on the western periphery. Of the Continental Great Powers, France had had an overseas Empire, and had lost much of it largely because of the inability of the structure of the French State to adapt itself to imperial tasks; Spain and Portugal still retained Empires, but precariously. It was England and Holland that gave the world an example of the close link that could exist between home politics and overseas commerce. They were to the seventeenth and eighteenth centuries what Venice and Genoa had been to the age of the crusades. The English reader will hardly need to be told how different was English society in the "age of Johnson" from the societies of France or Spain, Russia or Austria. Administration and politics took on a different colour from the different societies in which they functioned. The fact that power in England meant primarily sea-power, and hence something closely related to maritime enterprise was itself bound to create differences when compared with countries forced to divert men and money from productive work to drilling and the building of land fortifications. But if a symbol of the contrast is to be looked for, the bank-note will do as well as any. Public credit in a country like the Russia of Catherine the Great was created by the fiat of the ruler. Russian paper-money was acceptable because the State was stable but it bore no genuine relation to savings. In England and Holland, credit was created as the result of commercial enter-prise and could be commanded by governments enjoying the confidence of the commercial classes. The link between public opinion and hence politics on the one hand and finance and administration of the other, was a close one, and one that could be productive in great strength. In this respect France which suffered throughout the eighteenth century from its deficient financial machinery was much closer to eastern Europe than to England.

In the seventeenh century England and Holland had waged war against each other for predominance in northern and colonial waters. But after the accession of William III to the English throne their policies ran closely parallel for more than half a century. The strain of the war with Louis XIV and that of maintaining the Dutch position as a Great Power thereafter was heavy; and a period of economic decline set in. In particular the Dutch monopoly of the carrying trade was broken into by Bremen, Hamburg and Denmark. But this process took time to make its effect felt, and meanwhile it was to some extent masked by the fact that Amsterdam retained its importance as a banking centre and was indeed of fundamental importance in the development of the British financial system. The capitalists of Amsterdam found that British government securities and bank-stock offered a higher rate of interest than did investment in native industry. As late as 1776 it was estimated by the British Prime Minister, Lord North, that three-sevenths of the British national debt was held in Holland. Dutchmen also lent money privately in England on mortgage, and after 1750 in the British sugar islands of the West Indies. Also important was the fact that exchange transactions were so largely carried on through Amsterdam, and in Dutch money; there was for instance no direct rate for exchanging British and Russian currency despite the importance of Anglo-Russian trade in the eighteenth century. In the great wars of the middle of the century, it was through Dutch financial houses that Britain paid for continental armies. Despite the Orange restoration in 1747, a certain coldness set in latterly between Holland and England as the pro-French "patriot" party rose to power, but the interlocking of the two financial systems continued until the fourth Anglo-Dutch war of 1780 when Holland's consequent vulnerability was dramatically revealed.

The British political system of the eighteenth century, an oligarchy with certain popular elements, was one which faithfully reflected the existing distribution of wealth and social prestige, and thus secured at least the passive acquiescence of the overwhelming part of the people. Despite the advanced nature of the British economy and financial organization and the country's relative tolerance in matters of religion, English institutions retained some impress of an earlier age. The power of important privileged groups, while less clearly marked in law than on the Continent, was still the main feature of politics. Serfdom had long been a thing of the past, as was its economic counterpart, labour-services. The manor, where it existed, was an economic and social unit rather than an administrative one.

But what the owners of the land had lost as individuals they had on the whole retained as a class. The system of justices of the peace gave them almost unchallenged control of local government, and of the local administration of justice: where such things as the game-laws were concerned this was not unimportant. Controlling the militia, they had no cause to fear that the State might use the small standing army to their disadvantage, the less in that the latter was officered from their midst. To some extent the common division between the great magnates with their readier access to political influence and commercial affluence and the rural squirearchy existed in England also, and was not without its effect on the parliamentary scene. But the land was a unifying factor too great for the split to develop dangerously.

More unusual and more important were the intimate links between land on the one hand, and commerce and finance on the other. The fertilization of the countryside by commercial, professional and industrial wealth was no new thing; and with the expansion of industry and the growth of London, mineral royalties and rents began to be the reality behind the fortunes of some members of what looked like a true landed aristocracy.

It was the unity of interests of those with property, rather than the paper guarantees won from the Stuart monarchs and confirmed by the accession of the House of Hanover, that made it impossible for any English ruler to contemplate a despotism on the continental model. Those who believed that economic progress and social justice could only be obtained by authoritarian methods had no reason to admire English institutions, and their continental vogue was among would-be conservatives such as Montesquieu rather than among the radicals of the next generation. A characteristic feature of these institutions was the difficulty of drawing a clear line between public and private interests. Bodies like the Bank of England and the East India Company served both; the battles among the stockholders of the latter, and the fight for fortunes in India out of which these arose, were directly reflected in Parliament, and in the last resort decided there. The business of Parliament was again both public and private—the latter exemplified in the private enclosure bills by which the agrarian revolution was carried through. So too, although the public service possessed a core of permanent devoted and quasi-professional employees in such departments as the admiralty and the board of trade, it also offered many sinecures that were no more than claims on the public purse, while both genuine offices and sinecures were regarded as the legitimate sphere of patronage, and as the proper cement of political association. The cry of corruption raised against Whig magnates and King in turn was normally the cry of those who regarded themselves as improperly excluded from sharing in these fruits.

There were two further reasons why England underwent no experience to correspond with the absolutisms of the Continent, at least not in the eighteenth century—the earlier age of Strafford and Laud is another story. The first reason was that some of the work which was done or attempted on the Continent had already been done or was unnecessary in England: England was already a single market with no restrictions on internal movement: its State Church did not depend on Rome: its monasteries had been dissolved, and their wealth allowed to circulate in the common pool. Social amelioration was taken care of, no doubt inadequately but by no means negligibly, by local regulation or private philanthropy, the latter spurred on as the century progressed by an increasing number of tender consciences. Learning had its Radcliffe and Sloane; charity, its Coram and Oglethorpe. In the second place, the system produced until late in the day few serious and irreconcilable critics. The established Church was deeply intertwined in its outlook, machinery and personnel with the landed classes, and had no need to fear disestablishment nor even disendowment at the hands of its patrons. Protestant dissent was the object of some discrimination, but not sufficient to cause it to challenge a regime under which its adherents were unhampered either in their worship or in their temporal pursuits. Roman Catholics were more seriously incommoded, but their numbers were small and they formed a cave rather than an opposition. The secular intellectuals lacked any serious reason for the disaffection with the existing order which so strongly affected their compeers in France. The press was relatively free—increasingly so—and patrons in all sections of the ruling class and in all political

parties could be found by the young writer of talent. He was not
the social equal of the magnates but he need not fear chastise-
ment from their lackeys. Despite the cosmopolitan nature of
eighteenth-century culture the differences in the circumstances
of its producers was profound. Compare the life of Voltaire
with that of Dr. Johnson, or imagine how Rousseau might
have turned out if like Burke, he had had a Rockingham.

Eighteenth-century England presents an idyllic picture
only to the sentimentalist. Brutality, vice and crime were
endemic in the squalor of parts of the metropolis: and poverty
in the countryside strained social peace in years of scarcity and
high prices. The criminal law was harsh, and harsh in execution.
The increasing wealth of the community did not benefit all
sections equally. By twentieth-century standards the age was
callous towards personal misfortune. But as a working political
system that of eighteenth-century England stands up to most
tests. The fact that it was to survive almost unchanged the deep
upheaval of the agricultural and industrial revolutions, the
revolutionary contagion of France, and the strain of the
revolutionary and Napoleonic wars, and then to undergo
without a formal breach with the past the democratic reforms
of the nineteenth century is eloquent enough.

The weaknesses of the English polity in the eighteenth
century were on the external side. The Tudors had done
their work well enough in Wales for no fear to be felt on that
side. With Scotland, the Union had been harder to maintain.
In the end the commercial opportunities and the personal
careers open within it had been sufficient to enlist the support
of the lowlands, and the highly artificial nature of the Scottish
representative system made that country's representatives in
Parliament the obedient servants of the government of the day.
In the highlands it was different. The clan system persisted there
as an increasingly uneasy anachronism not only in Britain but in
Europe. The rebellion of 1745, too frequently described in
terms of personal loyalties, should perhaps be interpreted as the
last desperate flicker of armed resistance to change: thereafter
the Government with the chiefs turned landed magnates as its
often willing accomplices, stamped out the clan system for good,
and subjected the highlands to the common discipline of a

unitary state. Ireland, however, remained conquered but unabsorbed. It presented a problem which bore certain resemblances with that with which Hungary presented the Habsburgs, but the problem was complicated by a greater bitterness in the religious divisions between the mass of the peasantry, the Presbyterian north-east, and the Anglican landowning class. It might have been possible, had political considerations alone been given weight, to have staked everything on strengthening the Protestant ascendancy so that it should identify its fortunes wholly with those of England: in that case Irish nationalism presumably might have been delayed like some of the peasant nationalisms of eastern Europe until the nineteenth or even the twentieth century. This could not be done because certain economic interests in England were determined to use their political power to prevent Irish competition. Thus right through the eighteenth century the national interests of Ireland as a whole were voiced by the enfranchised and in a sense alien minority, as for instance by Swift. Neither the increased legislative devolution of 1782, nor the legislative and commercial union of 1800, unaccompanied as it was by Catholic emancipation, provided a solution for the relations of the two countries: nor indeed has the subsequent century and a half provided one.

The Irish problem was an old one dating in one form or another almost to the very beginnings of English history: the American problem on the contrary was almost invisible at the beginning of the eighteenth century, and by its end was a foreign rather than a domestic one. In 1750, the British colonies on the North American mainland—the nucleus of the future United States—formed only part of a single overseas Empire, governed from London according to a single set of principles. (India was a thing apart.) It has been estimated that those so ruled, of many colours, and scattered over four continents, numbered some 15,000,000. The share of North America was perhaps 1,250,000, although its population was growing rapidly, by natural increase, by free or indentured immigration, and by the import of negro slaves. By the eve of independence in 1775, it may have reached 2,500,000; of these perhaps 1,300,000 persons (including 57,000 negroes) were to be found in the northern, New England group (Massachusetts, Connecticut, New Hampshire and Rhode Island) and in the middle group (New York, New Jersey, Pennsylvania and Delaware) and 1,200,000 (including 500,000 negroes) in the south (Virginia, Maryland, the Carolinas, and Georgia).

Of the thirty-one British overseas dependencies in 1750, twenty-one enjoyed some form of representative institution—all the thirteen colonies named, and eight islands in the Caribbean. The divisions among the three groups of the mainland colonies were genuine, the product of differences in origin, in geographical setting, in economic activity and social structure. Difficulties of inter-colonial communication were accentuated by the deeply seamed coastline, and local attachments were naturally far stronger than the notion of the Empire as a whole, to say nothing of America as opposed to Britain. The limitations which mountain and forest, as well as the French and their Indian allies, had placed upon a rapid movement into the interior had stimulated an intensive exploitation of the resources to hand, relatively close settlement, and a consequently rapid development of indigenous social and institutional forms.

By the middle of the eighteenth century the colonies had already experienced the common fate of colonies of settlement. They depended upon the export of staple products to a metropolitan area which was the principal source of credit, and this situation tended to create a standing lack of ready money for commercial purposes or for the meeting of fiscal obligations. Internally there were clashes of interest between older and newer sections, between creditor and debtor, between planter, farmer and trader, and in the south between master and slave. These struggles had tended to seek for expression within institutions brought from the old world or refashioned to meet the new environment. Despite pockets of foreign-language settlers, the dominant element in the American inheritance was still clearly English, as much in religion and culture, as in law, administration and politics.

The imperial policy of the home government had to take account of these facts as well as of certain principles of action which related to the Empire as a whole. It was held that the economic activities of the colonists should be such as to benefit at least some sections of the metropolitan population, and to compete with as few as possible of them, though it had been accepted that tobacco culture was a colonial affair and that this crop should not be developed in England. It was even more important that the colonies should be a source of strength and not of weakness in the conflicts between Britain and other Powers; naval stores must be provided. At the beginning, the idea of the colonies as a home for surplus population had been important; but after the middle of the seventeenth century it was accepted that under-population not over-population was England's national problem, and only the offscourings of society were encouraged or compelled to go overseas. Such policies did not seem tyrannical nor even unduly detrimental to the interests of the colonists. Looked at from London it seemed quite natural that the commerce of the colonies in most important products should be directed towards London for the benefit of its merchants and of its mercantile marine, the essential standby in time of war. The desire of the New Englanders to trade directly with foreign countries, as their own shipping became more important, or with foreign colonies in the Caribbean seemed selfishly to overlook the interests of the whole for the sake of the part. But a fairly lax administration of some of the relevant regulations helped to prevent the differences coming to a head.

In the same way, the political relationship that hammered itself out between the Glorious Revolution and the Seven Years' War was completely in accordance with the accepted British ideas on government. The raising of revenue for the defraying of local administrative charges was a matter for the colonists acting through representative institutions —institutions by no means without their element of oligarchy, but as suitable to the existing state of affairs in the colonies as those at Westminster were appropriate to England. The executive government was the Crown's affair and it was natural that posts in the colonies should, like posts in England, be filled by the operation of influence and patronage, rather than on any sterner basis. If fighting had to be done against the French and their allies, it was obvious that the regular officers of His Majesty's Forces should take precedence over the local leaders of raw colonial levies. If the European tactics of such officers proved unsuitable to the American forest, and led to disasters such as that which befell General Braddock in 1755, this was no good reason for challenging the established order of things. If the imperial government took the view that a hard currency should be maintained and opposed the demands of frontier inflationists, if it supported the claims of the holders of royal land-grants, colonial proprietors such as the Penn family, against those who took the New World view that the land belonged to those who could settle and work it, it was the result of adherence to principles which had proved sound enough in the home environment by men who had little or no experience of any other. The British North Americans of 1750 were not oppressed, and had no need to look with envy on the far more closely circumscribed subjects of the rival empires in the New World.

There was no inherent reason why the situation that existed in the middle of the eighteenth century should not have perpetuated itself. In some ways indeed the centrifugal tendencies within the system were becoming weaker. As trade and communication across the Atlantic increased, so did the stake of Britain and America and of individual British and American men of business in each other's welfare. Study by young Americans in Britain, the reading of English books, the adopting of English tastes and fashions as life for the wealthier became easier and more varied—all these tended to knit the ruling classes of the two countries into a single whole. The amount of American business coming before the privy council, the board of trade, the office of the secretary of state, the treasury, and other departments, as well as before Parliament itself led to the colonies retaining regular agents to speak for them in London. For the normal routine of affairs the existing machinery seemed adequate enough. It was war and victory that tilted the balance—war whose origins itself became a source of dispute, since Englishmen maintained that it had been fought to protect the Empire, while Americans held that they had been dragged into a purely European squabble.

Wars have to be paid for, and it seemed obvious enough

that the colonists should pay their share, though their unfavourable balance of payments made it difficult. Furthermore,
taxation for general purposes, as apart from duties designed to
regulate the movement of commodities, had not previously been
attempted by Parliament, and to attempt it was to raise awkward
questions. The reaction of the colonists showed that they had
not appreciated how fast England had moved towards substituting Parliamentary for monarchical rule. The colonists did
not dispute their allegiance to the Crown until they were
forced to do so by the realization that Crown and Parliament
were inseparable. They showed from the beginning of the dispute, both by their actions and by their arguments, that they
had been working on the implicit theory that their own
assemblies were almost co-equal with Parliament, that they
could not be taxed nor legislated for by a Parliament in which
they were unrepresented. The colonists would have denied the
familiar gibe that the British constitution does not exist: they
were sure it existed and they were sure they knew what it was.
An attempt was made to reach a compromise by drawing an
awkward distinction between direct taxation and internal
law-making on the one hand, and matters of imperial interest
on the other, and by consenting that Parliament should continue to deal with the matter. If tempers had been better kept,
and all Englishmen had been as far-sighted as the wisest of
them, this might have served for a time; but it was inherently
unworkable as a permanent solution. Once the colonists had
developed a local leadership with sufficient skill to frame the
issue—and their apprenticeship in the colonial and local
governments had powerfully contributed to its development—
only four possibilities were open. The fundamental position of
the colonists could be accepted, and they could be given
complete self-government as members of a free association of
communities under a single Crown—the modern Commonwealth idea. But this demanded a stage of development in the
colonies, and a maturity of political understanding on both
sides which had not been reached. Alternatively some form of
federal solution was called for. This in fact, meant, to begin
with, representation of the colonies at Westminster, a thing
hardly practicable in the age of sail. If these were ruled out, then

either Parliament must make good its claim to sovereignty throughout the Crown's dominions, and treat all colonial institutions as enjoying merely delegated powers, however extensive these might be, or else, the colonists must claim total independence, and make good this claim in theory, and by the sword.

If the issues involved had been restricted to taxation and trade, the struggle might not have come so soon. But the results of the war of 1763 were not confined to an attempt to keep the land-tax in England down by securing revenue in the colonies. The conquest of Canada and Florida meant that British imperialism had passed from a mercantile to a territorial phase. Much has been made of the fact that by removing the fear of French aggression, the British victory freed the colonists from their previous need for protection, and so made them readier to question the necessity of an imperial tie that now seemed productive of burdens rather than of benefits. It is equally important that the conquest of Canada and Florida was itself unwelcome to them. The increase in the area of the Empire would, it was held, depreciate the value of the original colonies, and their products, and would disperse their population. Used to despotic rule, these colonies would be the mere tools of the home government, and could be used to coerce the true Americans—we might think of Canada as England's Bohemia. Protestant bigotry deplored the toleration that Britain showed to her new subjects. Above all, the proclamation of 1763 holding up trans-Appalachian settlement while a new Indian policy was worked out, was directly opposed to powerful American interests involved in land-settlement and land-speculation. The Quebec Act of 1774 by extending the boundaries of Canada to the south suggested that the interests of the Canadian fur-trader were to be given preference over those of the American settler. The Indians were to be protected, and the farmers abandoned to their brutal assaults. The clash of policies appeared from London to be one of enlightened imperialism against a series of unrelated local greeds and pretensions. From the American side it increasingly took on the appearance of a national movement provoked into resistance by wanton tyranny. The latter view has tended to dominate our histories. Both, however, contain elements of distortion.

The imperial view was never universally held in Britain and the American cause never lacked supporters particularly from among those opposed on other grounds to the King and ministry. On the American side unanimity was even further off. The internal divisions within the colonies were too profound for any cause to unite all sections; many preferred the rule of Parliament to that of the locally dominant group. In the propertied classes, men like the wealthy merchants of Philadelphia and the larger landowners in the Middle Colonies certainly wished to maintain the British connexion, as did the Anglican clergymen, and indeed Anglicans generally. The radical elements in the New England towns and among the farmers were too weak to dominate the scene when the struggle began over the Sugar Act of 1764 and the Stamp Act of 1765. The theme of the next decade is essentially that of their acquisition of new leaders, largely from among the plantation-owners of Virginia. To what extent the increasing economic difficulties which this class faced as a result partly of soil-exhaustion, and in particular their increasing indebtedness, led to their being ready to take up the rôle of revolutionaries for which they seemed so unfitted, has never been satisfactorily explained but that these difficulties were important there can be no doubt. By 1775 such men had much to gain and little to lose; and they made a successful revolution possible. Every revolution has its intellectuals and these were provided by the New England and Philadelphian lawyers, and by men who though not primarily lawyers were nevertheless trained in law, like Thomas Jefferson. But what distinguished the American Revolution was that its leadership was so largely in the hands of practical men of affairs: no one could be less like the conventional picture of the dis-affected intellectual than George Washington. And it is for this reason perhaps that unlike most other revolutions, this one stopped more or less where its original leaders wished it to.

It is a common error to confuse the American Revolution with the American War of Independence. The American Revolution on its political side was achieved when the Continental Congress dominated by the temporary alliance of Virginia and Massachusetts decided to raise an army, and to put its dispute with the imperial government to the arbitrament of force. It meant that the party which believed in resistance was strong enough to feel able to coerce its opponents at home, and act as though it represented a nation—a nation hitherto unknown to the world. It continued as a movement inside the former colonies (now States) whose object was to remodel their institutions in accordance with their new status, and in a generally democratic direction. Whether the War of Independence was to succeed or not was on the other hand, a diplomatic and military question and was settled on the international plane.

One cannot, of course, altogether separate the two things. The Declaration of Independence came as early in the struggle as it did, largely because foreign recognition and foreign aid seemed to depend on the Americans' breaking down all the bridges that might lead back to a reconciliation. But for the European rulers the war was merely a renewal of the old struggle against the overweening power of Britain. France gave vital assistance to the rebels, first surreptitiously and then as an open ally: Spain lured by the vain hope of winning back Gibraltar, did so with greater reluctance, rightly fearing the effect of a successful revolution in one part of the western hemisphere upon the temper of the other. Holland deeply divided internally, was dragged in by the anti-British feelings of the Republican opponents of the Orangists, and by the refusal of the Amsterdam merchants to abandon the profitable trade with the French. Although the Dutch colonies lost to Britain were restored in the general peace-making, the war marked the real ruin of the Republic which now depended on others for the defence of its colonial trade. The challenge to British sea power and to its right to interfere with neutral shipping went outside the circle of the active belligerents. In 1780, Catherine of Russia signed the declaration which established the terms of the League of Armed Neutrality, a group of powers pledged to insist on a narrow interpretation of contraband, and on the maximum freedom for neutral traffic. Sweden and Denmark as well as Russia armed their ships in order to enforce conformity with their demands: Prussia, Austria, Naples, and even Portugal, acceded to the declaration later. The Armed Neutrality was more effective indeed on paper than in practice: but the diplomatic isolation of England was complete.

The calculations of self-interest which governed foreign intervention in the war were equally to the fore in the negotiations which culminated in the Peace of Paris of 1783. Canada was unconquered, and with the British Caribbean islands, and the fruits of a new surge of mercantile expansion in the Indian Ocean and the Pacific, remained as one of the foundation-stones of a second British Empire. The Americans who had been willing to see the French assist them to repel the English attempt at a reconquest did not wish to see themselves too closely confined in their borders by a re-established French empire in North America. The arrival of the Spaniards in Louisiana in 1763 and their return to Florida in 1783 raised the question of the Mississippi valley in a new form and with it the whole question of the future destiny of the new United States.

Outside the North American continent the changes brought about by the peace were scarcely commensurate with the effort involved in the prosecution of the war. Florida and Minorca did not satisfy Spain. Louisiana and various trading posts in India and West Africa, even when combined with the blow to Britain's power and prestige involved in accepting the fact of American independence, were inadequate compensation to the French for the major blow inflicted upon their national solvency. The most direct connexion between the American and French Revolutions lay in the fact that it was French expenditure in the war that produced the financial impasse that led to the calling of the States-General in 1789.

It would be wrong, however, to think that this was the only connexion. French officers who had fought in America came back enthusiastic for the ideals which they believed the Americans to have upheld: the prestige of Lafayette is eloquent on this point. And European enthusiasm for the Americans was not confined to France. In England itself, shaken as it was by war and defeat, radicalism made important strides until its progress was cut short by the national reaction against the excesses and aggressiveness of revolutionary France. In Holland the prestige of American republicanism contributed to the

turbulence of the political scene before the restoration of the
Orangists by Prussian arms and under British patronage, in
1787. Even Germany was affected. This was largely due to the
sale to Britain by the German princelings of soldiers for the war.
But even apart from this, the claims of the colonists seem to
have received a ready hearing especially among intellectuals.
In Spanish America the aspirations of the creoles received a new
impetus: Miranda was talking revolution with North American
leaders in 1783. It has been rightly argued that the Americans
were in fact less interested in universal notions of rights than in
their specific claims as inheritors of English constitutional
privileges, that their field of vision was limited to their own
affairs, that the Declaration of Independence itself is a limited
document relying on specific grievances to justify its radical
conclusions. If this were the whole truth, the international
repercussions of the Americans' success would be difficult to
understand. At a time when many rulers were exercising compulsion against sections of their subjects, why should the wrongs
of the American colonists excite so much interest, particularly
since no great questions of religion or nationality were seemingly
involved but rather a series of material disputes over taxes, land-
claims and tariff restrictions? The provisional answer to such
questions must be sought in two directions, in the development
of a political philosophy and of a social myth.

The colonists had indeed begun by an appeal to British
constitutional practice and to their rights as Englishmen.
But as it became apparent that even sympathizers with their
grievances, such as Chatham, would make no concessions on
the point of Parliament's ultimate sovereignty, they shifted
their ground to the more universal one of natural rights.
In England, natural rights as they appeared in the individualist
philosophy of John Locke were now regarded generally as being
adequately guaranteed by the enforced dependence of the
executive on Parliament: for the Americans they implied the
right to reject the authority of a Parliament in which they
were unrepresented. The sophistries of "virtual representation"
(urged against English reformers as well) went for nothing:
the King had tried to set up an absolute tyranny: Parliament
had endeavoured to "extend an unwarrantable jurisdiction".

The just powers of governments, in the language of the Declaration of Independence, derived "from the consent of the governed", and no prescriptive rights or duties could stand in the way of "the right of the people to alter or abolish" one form of government and to set up a new one "laying its foundation on such principles and organizing its powers in such form, as to them shall seem most likely to effect their safety and happiness". Therefore King and Parliament must be thrust aside, and replaced by something new.

The idea of natural rights was no novelty in western political thinking: it had been argued before that a ruler who ignored them had in some sense broken the contract upon which the allegiance of his subjects was based. What was new was the idea that natural rights might be thought of as a perpetual yardstick for the judgement of governments, that the people, the community at large, could simply decide that a particular form of government was not meeting this test, and throw it over with as little compunction as a man might sell a horse that no longer served his purposes. Natural rights in this context meant a perpetual right of revolution, it meant denying the divinity that had hitherto hedged not only kings but all constituted authorities. This was heady wine and not only Americans would get drunk upon it.

It is significant that this point was not overlooked by contemporaries of these events themselves. "The Americans," wrote Josiah Tucker "are now Mr. Locke's disciples: who has laid down such maxims in his Treatise on Government, that if they were to be executed according to the letter and in the manner the Americans pretend to understand them, they would necessarily unhinge and destroy every Government upon earth". With equal vehemence Tom Paine proclaimed the universality of the new American ideals: "O ye that love mankind: Ye that dare oppose, not only the tyranny stand forth: every spot of the old world is overrun with oppression. Freedom hath been hunted round the globe. Asia and Africa, have long expelled her —Europe regards her like a stranger, and England hath given her warning to depart. O! receive the fugitive, and prepare in time an asylum for mankind".

This asylum was to be more than political. The political

appeal of the new country was less potent than the social one. It was not simply that people were asked to regard the United States as having a political system in which the people truly ruled themselves, it was not just that the political inheritance of the past had been seemingly obliterated, what really counted was that social inequality existed no longer. In this new world no-one was concerned to assert that he was better than his fellow: no-one bowed the knee to birth or wealth or learning: all were stripped naked before the majesty of a continent to be conquered: the conflicts of races and classes that had covered Europe with battlefields and Bastilles gave way to a joint enterprise, the subduing of physical nature. The vogue of Benjamin Franklin in the *salons* of pre-revolutionary Paris was not an accident: his homespun clothes and manners, his provincial shrewdness and above all his patriarchal simplicity fitted precisely into the picture which the intellectuals had drawn of the natural man, free of the vices of sophisticated society. The idea of the "noble savage" had done good work in social criticism, but, close up, the real savage was rather a disappointment: the American pioneer would serve much better. Europeans could read Crèvecœur on "what is then the American? the American is a new man, who acts upon new principles: he must therefore entertain new ideas and form new opinions. From involuntary idleness, servile dependence, penury, and useless labour, he has passed to toils of a different nature, rewarded by ample subsistence. This is an American". They might or might not want to go to America; if they could read, the odds were that they would not go. What they did want, was to see these American phenomena reproduced at home. The European wanted his America, his free, egalitarian society in Europe; the American social myth had thus added a new and powerful ingredient to the revolutionary cauldron.

CHAPTER VIII

ABSOLUTISM IN TRANSFORMATION: 1789–1815

THE history of ideas is not identical with the history of institutions. Even the political doctrines of the revolutionary Americans were reconciled with the establishment of what proved a permanent and stable system of government; and profound changes in the geographical and social outlook were necessary before the subsequent swing towards the more radical Jacksonian democracy became possible. Nor were the ideas of the Jacksonians, to say nothing of those of Jefferson or Paine, themselves radical, by comparison for instance with those ventilated in England at the crisis of the seventeenth-century revolution. For a parallel to this earlier ferment of ideas about the recasting of human society we must turn to France, though there these ideas were advanced on secular rather than on religious grounds. One could go further, and say that if one takes continental Europe as a whole, and can set off German romanticism and nationalism against the universalist ideologies of France, almost every social and political idea with which the twentieth century has been confronted can claim legitimate or illegitimate ancestry within the crowded quarter of a century after 1789. What is surprising is that so much in Europe's institutional equipment managed to survive and be passed on into the next period of its history.

The essential continuity of the history of the continental countries was broken neither by the irruption of new ideas, nor by the recasting of the map of Europe through war, on a scale altogether incommensurate with the changes which have been chronicled for the preceding century. Similarly the very different institutions through which eighteenth-century England had carried on its affairs survived the violent economic upheaval of the industrial revolution almost intact, and were only gradually reformed to suit its purposes in the course of the fifty years after 1830.

At first sight the contrast between maritime and continental powers, and on the Continent, between West and East, was no less marked after the revolutionary wave had passed and subsided than it had been before it. Indeed after 1830, the diplomatic constellation itself seemed to reflect the antagonisms between constitutional and absolutist governments. But, as has earlier been suggested, this is partly an illusion. For a relatively short period of time the demands of the State in the West were curtailed by the economic theory of *laissez-faire* which was found congenial by the entrepreneurial classes at a particular juncture in the history of capitalism. But this did not mean that the State was weaker than it had been in the age of mercantilist absolutism. In the skill and devotion of its administrators, in its ability to command obedience and to tap national resources for public ends, the nineteenth-century state was almost everywhere stronger than its eighteenth-century predecessor; the very inventions that helped produce the new capitalist wealth —the railway, the telegraph, the power-driven printing press— were all conducive to the affirmation of central authority; for one thing, administrators could now acquire accurate information to an extent hitherto inconceivable. Furthermore, the spread of education, everywhere an inseparable accompaniment of technical and economic progress, gave greater opportunities for new political creeds to arise, and to fill the emotional void seemingly created by the decline of religious certainties and the greater social instability. Such secular ideologies might take a democratic form and appear as a continuation of the eighteenth-century protest against all forms of privilege, though it took the genius of Tocqueville to perceive as early as the 1830s the full lineaments of the levelling democracy of the future. Or they might take the form of a national or even a racial justification of the State's purposes, and invest acceptance of its demands with the traditional veneration accorded to patriotism. A State which could claim neither democratic nor national justification like Austria, would inevitably continue to lead a precarious life. Nevertheless, it took the cataclysm of the First World War to write *finis* to the Habsburg Empire. Even

Czarist Russia where the Government disdained all ideological support, where the gap between the Government and the masses remained almost unbridged, survived until finally crushed by military defeat and the ensuing economic dislocation. The powerful edifice of the French monarchy that Louis XVI inherited from his predecessors apparently crumbled to pieces as the result of a train of events set in motion by the unsolved fiscal problems arising from the American wars; the Romanov Empire fell only when millions of lives had been sacrificed; and when it did so, it brought down its two rivals to destruction with it. Upon the ruins of these three Empires there arose in our own day states making still greater demands upon their citizens, and exercising absolutisms more all-embracing than any hitherto known.

It is perhaps worth calling attention once more to the geographical contrasts which underlie so much of European history; for the modern conflict of ideologies between western Liberalism and Socialist Absolutism, whether in its Nazi or Communist form, can only properly be understood if these are kept in mind. It is in western Europe with its various and many-sided social life that the ravages of political totalitarianism have been most firmly resisted; it is only where society itself has produced new institutions, or where older ones successfully resisted the absolutist monarchs of the eighteenth century and their revolutionary successors that one can still perceive that tension between the State and society which is the condition of a healthy political life.

If the State is not omnipotent and omnicompetent in the North Atlantic democracies as it is, for instance, in Soviet Russia, this cannot be ascribed solely to constitutional guarantees, whether of the American written variety, or enshrined in accepted constitutional practice as in Britain. It is much more important that in these countries new independent agglomerations of power have replaced the privileged groups of the eighteenth century. Whether it be a business corporation, a trade union, the regional or national cohesiveness of some minority group, a church, a professional organization, or a university, the existence of such an independent focus of authority and loyalty involves a limitation upon the absolutism of the State. Indeed, there is no method of establishing limits upon power other than the setting up of power to rival it. Except in the smallest of possible political communities—the original Swiss forest cantons, for instance—the individual cannot possibly count for anything in political society. He can only exert influence through his membership of a group; the descent from feudalism through Whiggism to Liberalism is a much more honourable one than is often admitted.

It is not true, of course, that this tension between the State and society should normally show itself in open conflict. For it would be intolerable if political life were the scene of constant struggles between the central power and important social groups. British society would long ago have foundered if every generation had needed a Simon de Montfort or a John Hampden. In a healthy political order, every group that has something to contribute to society will be in a position to do so. Its separate identity and capacity for resistance will be held in reserve. It is only when important sections of the population feel that they are being frustrated by an existing order which the relevant political authority is unable or unwilling to see altered, that a revolutionary crisis develops. It is the alienation of vital elements that is fatal. This does not need a thorough-going absolutism for it to happen; we have noted a crisis of this kind in colonial America. But an absolutism makes it more likely because, it will inevitably tend to adapt itself too slowly to a social order that can never itself remain static.

France in the eighteenth century, provides the classic instance; but it would be wrong to restrict the field of our observations. In Prussia, for instance, there was the inevitable reaction after the death of Frederick II; some of his character-istic administrative devices were abandoned; but these changes were relatively superficial. More significant was the fact that the ideas of the enlightenment continued to penetrate the adminis-tration through its recruitment from the middle-class students of the universities, while at the same time, the nobles remained supreme at Court, in the army and above all on their own estates. The weakness of this duality in social outlook and inspiration was to make itself felt when the Frederician military inheritance was found wanting at Jena. It continued to frustrate the would-be reformers of Prussia after this national humiliation, and was only resolved, and then in quite different circumstances, after 1848. There was also another factor in the Prussian situation. The increase of the bourgeois element in the administration was not rapid enough to take up all the output of the universities; growing centralization, particularly at the expense of the cities, actually cut down the number of posts available. As a consequence, there grew up in late eighteenth-century Prussia a class of disaffected intellectuals, for whom the absolutist system seemed too closely bound up with the privileges of the nobility to be worth their allegiance. Social criticism here did not need the French Revolution to set it off; and it was from such roots as these that there were born visions of a wider national community in which the creative urges thus frustrated could be harnessed. Hence arose German romanticism with its highly charged national colouring. But although German nationalism was the product in part of individual discontents, it took on an essentially collective form. What these people wanted was not to do away with the State, but to enlarge it. In as far as men like Fichte proclaimed the desirability of a self-sufficient and integrated national community, they were, in a sense, translating into nineteenth-century terms some of the objectives of the enlightened despots. The State would now embody the national will. It was, rather belatedly, the depersonalization of the enlightened despot, and this tendency had already been manifest before the Revolution in a more advanced country like France.

The French scene in the pre-Revolutionary period was a more complicated one. The pressures upon the State were more various, the number of the alienated more considerable. There was a growing movement towards economic individualism, both in commerce and on the land—struggling in the former case against relics of State control and State-supported monopoly, and in the latter against the surviving customary restrictions on the utilization of the soil. Free trade was the slogan of one movement; enclosure of the other.

A programme along these lines was theoretically within the scope of the existing political authorities; the royal power could have been thrown, as the physiocrats wished it to be, on the side of freedom in economic life. Under men who were, like Turgot open to the ideas of the enlightenment, attempts were indeed made along these lines; but the vested interests opposed to change were on the whole too strong for them; and an alliance between the French Crown and the commercial middle classes was never consolidated. Indeed there was, towards the end, something of an aristocratic reaction. The attack on privilege by men of property which was the essence of the first stage in the French Revolution was thus understandable; the desired revision of the laws could only be attained by the employment of new political means.

But the idea of sweeping political and social changes had to be conceived and diffused before power could be grasped and used in this way. From this point of view, it is the attack on the intellectual defences of absolutism that is the most important part of the Revolution's prehistory. In the first half of the eighteenth century, this attack was largely directed against the regime's clerical support, and against the whole edifice of religious orthodoxy. A monarchy by divine right was an anachronism in a world rapidly absorbing and crudely interpreting, the amazing advances of the natural sciences, and after about 1750, this original battle was won. Having won it, many reformers still placed their hopes on the Crown, still felt that the *philosophes* could replace the expelled Jesuits as keepers of the royal conscience. But discussion and speculation had created a public for discussion and speculation; the French ruling classes who had been taught to be sceptical about God were not prepared to dogmatize about anything else, and the spirit of inquiry pursued mundane paths which soon left no temporal institution uncriticized.

This outburst of abstract theorizing forms so startling a contrast with the quiescence of preceding ages, that some have been content to regard the French Revolution as a simple plot through which men, possessed of a series of general ideas about politics, seized the State, and proceeded to put their ideas into effect. The truth is more subtle than that; but the course which the Revolution took would hardly have been possible if the new ideology, and the new political language in which it was cast, had not provided an intelligible framework for the conflicts which it engendered.

In some respects it was more important that men should talk and write with this new freedom, than they should express particular ideas. Their ideas were indeed diverse and of unequal importance and relevance. But from the point of view of the future they had one great common denominator; they amounted to a virtual denial not so much of the existing political order, as of its human and social presuppositions. Instead of a God-ordained society they spoke of reason; instead of regarding sin as inherent in man, they pinned their faith to human perfecti-bility and believed that education could remould the human personality; instead of the privileges of the different orders, they insisted upon egalitarianism; in a society deeply infused with militarism, they despised the martial qualities, in an age of dynastic aggrandizement they extolled fraternity among the peoples.

Of all these the most far-reaching in its implications was the belief in human goodness. For when men brought up on such ideas had seen so much of this original programme achieved with scarcely any genuine resistance from the pillars of the old order, they came to believe that they possessed the secret of human happiness and could legislate for it. Those who opposed them could only be doing so because they were irredeemably corrupt, and therefore they should be swept away. Virtue and corruption might be envisaged differently by Robespierre on the one hand, and Babeuf on the other; but what they had in common was a belief in the objective existence of such categories among men.

The State which the early achievements of the Revolution seemed for a time to be weakening, now emerged as the instru-ment of the new social engineering. Indeed it was stronger than it had ever been. The old confused mass of overlapping adminis-trative units and jurisdictions went the way of other reminders of a provincial and feudal past. It was succeeded by the new uniformity of the "departments" into which France was now divided. But it was not simply that administration was tightened up; the organization of the virtuous in local political clubs gave added strength to the emissaries of the Republican Government.

In these can be seen the embryo of the modern totalitarian one-party State. The Jacobin absolutism claimed more, and took more, than the royal absolutism that had been swept away. Not only internal enemies but external opponents of the new ideas were guilty of treason; for revolutionary France claimed a new sense of national community, and better right to "natural frontiers". Wars fought to aggrandize revolutionary France were not open to the charge of militarism, since they were ostensibly fought to liberate.

The conquest of power by a new clan or group which is the essence of all Revolutions, alters the outlook of its conquerors, and tends to make them fall back in some respects upon the tried institutions of the past. For Robespierre and his associates the opportunity for consolidation did not arrive; too many interests had been alienated, the foundations of their power were altogether too narrow, for their rule to last. The further development of the essential theoretical basis of democratic absolutism went on in an underworld removed from the real hope of power. In the Communist notions of Babeuf, and above all in his belief that professional government is unnecessary, that any citizen can perform the simple tasks involved in running the community's affairs, that dictatorship is only transitional and must move towards a society which an identity of interests and sentiments will suffice to preserve, the modern totalitarian utopianism of a Lenin is substantially prefigured. But for the time being, power in France passed into other hands and eventually, and perhaps inevitably, into those of a soldier-ruler.

The rôle of Napoleon was an essential one in the transformation of absolutism. For he showed both what could, and what could not, be carried on from the previous age. His ideas on domestic policy were not substantially different from those of the enlightened despots; if one were to call him the French Frederick the Great one would not be doing him a substantial injustice. His object, like Frederick's, was a country whose resources were in their entirety available to its ruler. But the new absolutism should succeed where the French monarchy had failed. The Revolution had completed the downfall of that traditional French aristocracy, which the monarchy itself had done its best for so long to exclude from active participation in political life. This verdict would not be reversed; nor would the other privileged classes of the older France be revived. The men of money, the *parvenus* who had come to the fore under the Directory and Empire, were not powerful enough to be feared. The administration was to be wholly professional, and wholly dependent upon the Government; national credit should at last be assured through a new Bank of France; above all a national system of education, the University, should see to it that Frenchmen were trained for their appropriate rôle in the new social hierarchy, and given an official creed as the solid foundation of their thinking. Within so rigid a framework, one could afford to put an end to the revolutionary quarrel with the Church which some had found so painful; the Church, shorn of its pretensions, could become a bastion of the new social order. Now that feudalism was abolished for good, now that Frenchmen were to be equal before the law, and given also that State intervention in economic life could henceforth substantially be limited to regulating external commerce, revolutionary ideas on the one hand, and reactionary hankerings on the other, could be disregarded. They were an affair of cliques, a police rather than a political problem. The Napoleonic system gave every promise of stability. And, shorn of the Emperor, it fulfilled the promise. Many of the fundamental institutions of the Fourth Republic are still Napoleonic though once again, economic and social change has made them increasingly anachronistic.

For those who had lived through the French Revolution, the realization that the State had increased its power, that the individualism of the original Declaration of Rights of 1789 was a passing phase was unacceptable. Most of all was this so, for those who had seen it as a continuation of the struggle in America. Napoleon was on St. Helena, and the brother of Louis XVI ruled a France from which many ancient landmarks had disappeared when, on 10th December, 1817, Lafayette wrote to Jefferson a letter which later generations may well find supremely ironic:

"Politics as you justly observe have ever been our hobby.

Oppressed as they are in this European wrong side of the Atlantic, they are not so desperate as one might mourn them. The 11th July, 1789 Declaration of Rights, which has been honoured with your approbation is still the creed of an immense majority in France and elsewhere; nor is it possible for any party or dynasty in this and other countries to hope for duration out of the circle which it has traced out. Napoleon, an uncommon man, found means for some years to escape under a revolutionary mask and a heap of laurels. Nobody now in France can stand it so long; no court in Europe could last for two generations of divine right. The principle of national instead of special governments is working under the bed of lies which the Sainte Alliance are holding over the European world."

Lafayette was right in the sense that to try to restore the *ancien régime* and its theoretical sanctions was impossible. National governments—governments putting forward a claim to represent the community as a whole—would replace special governments, those of a dynasty or privileged class. But this would mean not less but more government. Power at the service of a community would be more effective and would be applied more ruthlessly than power at the service of an individual monarch. The wars of the Revolutionary and Napoleonic period had given a foretaste of what this might mean. One can endeavour to discount their novelty by references to France's age-long quest for suitable frontiers; but in fact, the Napoleon's summons to his army to go forward and live on the accumulated wealth which the long peace and the piety of religious and, latterly, of artistic pilgrims had brought to Italy, was a naked appeal to the right of the stronger such as the previous age had on the whole tried to avoid. Here again, one must not sentimentalize over the *ancien régime*; the partitions of Poland were no less immoral than the destruction of Venetian independence. But it is true that nationalism proved as inimical as religion to any notion of humanizing war. The Peninsular War as seen by Goya was as horrible as the Thirty Years' War as seen by Callot. And war, and preparations for war, were to be as central to the new absolutisms as to the old.

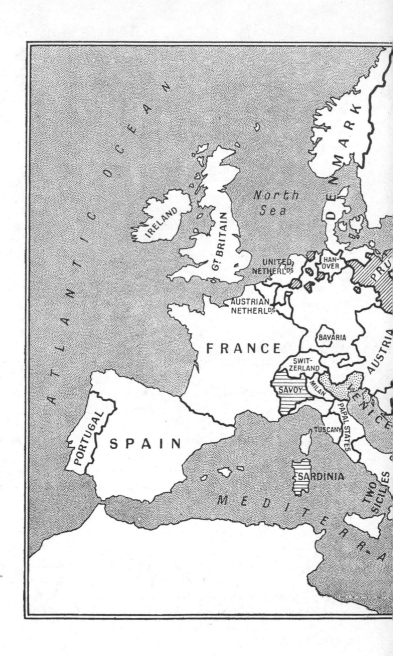

THE GREAT POWERS
OF EUROPE : 1789
Prussia ▨ Sardinia ☰
Venice ▨
0   200   400 MILES

DEN

RUSSIA

OLAND

NGARY

Caspian Sea

Black Sea

OTTOMAN EMPIRE

AN SEA

"GEOGRAPHIA" LTD.

Lafayette was still thinking of the Revolution as a blow against absolutism; we are more likely to think of the impediments to absolutism which it helped to remove. These impediments were to a great extent institutional; but they were also ideal. To understand what went wrong, one has to re-examine the claims of the *philosophes* and the programme of the enlightenment. The human evils which they rebelled against were genuine evils; serfdom in one form or another, the denial of human dignity, an ostentation of luxury at odds with an economic order which left so many so needy—all these were part and parcel of the society which eighteenth-century absolutism upheld. But the notion that State action could sweep these evils away, that Power would be used for beneficent purposes as easily as it had hitherto been perverted for selfish ones was proved to be based on a misunderstanding either of human beings or of the nature of social cohesion, or of both. Neither the heirs of the enlightenment nor the reactionaries against it have yet explained precisely what went wrong. The history of absolutism is only just beginning to be written.

A NOTE ON BOOKS

The period we have been dealing with has been endlessly studied, but many of the books on it are not primarily concerned with the particular aspects that we have chosen to emphasize, and access to those that are is limited by language barriers. A good guide to the whole period and to the literature about it will be found in the relevant volumes of the American historical series, "The Rise of Modern Europe" edited by W. L. Langer. These are: F. L. Nussbaum, *The Triumph of Science and Reason*, 1660–85 (1953); J. B. Wolf, *The Emergence of the Great Powers*, 1685–1715 (1951); P. Roberts, *The Quest for Security*, 1715–40 (1947); W. L. Dorn, *Competition for Empire*, 1740–63 (1940); L. Gershoy, *From Despotism to Revolution*, 1763–89 (1944); Crane Brinton, *A Decade of Revolution*, 1789–99 (1934); G. Bruun, *Europe and the French Imperium* (1938). The volumes by Dorn and Gershoy are particularly valuable from the point of view of this book. The period is also covered in volumes X to XIV of the French series, "Peuples et Civilizations" edited by L. Halphen and Ph. Sagnac, now being reissued in a second edition. The underlying economic philosophy and practice of the period received its classic treatment in Eli Heckscher, *Mercantilism* (London, 1935). An unusual attempt at a comparative study is provided in the symposium, *The European Nobility in the Eighteenth Century*, edited by A. Goodwin (1953). For the rest it is necessary to have recourse to works on particular countries. On French institutions, Ph. Sagnac, *La Formation de la Société Française Moderne* (Vol. 1, 1945, Vol. 2, 1947) and F. Olivier-Martin, *Histoire du Droit Français* (1948), have been valuable. On Belgium, too neglected in the text, there is H. Pirenne, *Histoire de Belgique*, Vols. V, VI (1921–6); on Germany see W. H. Bruford, *Germany in the Eighteenth Century* (1952). On Spain there is for those who do not read Spanish, the great work of G. Desdevises du Dezert, "L'Espagne de l'Ancien Régime", in *Revue Hispanique*, Vols. LXIV, LXX, LXXIII.

B. H. Sumner, *Survey of Russian History* (1944) and J. Rutkowski, *Histoire Economique de la Pologne avant les Partages* (1927) are of immense value for eastern Europe. So, too, is H. Marczali, *Hungary in the Eighteenth Century* (1910); R. J. Kerner, *Bohemia in the Eighteenth Century* (Berkeley, California, 1932), while full of information is poorly arranged. S. K. Padover, *The Revolutionary Emperor: Joseph II* (1934), is very helpful. Interesting as an example of new trends in the study of the period is H. Brunschwig, *La Crise de l'Etat Prussien à la fin du XVIII siècle* (1947). For the British background to the American Revolution see C. M. Andrews, *The Colonial Period of American History*, Vol. IV (Yale 1938) and V. T. Harlow, *The Founding of the Second British Empire*, Vol. I (1952). The sources for the interpretation I have given to it here are indicated in my book *Thomas Jefferson and American Democracy* (1948) and in my collection of documents *The Debate on the American Revolution* (1950).

The period from 1789 to 1815 belongs more properly to other volumes in this series; but I must acknowledge my debt to the writings on it of J. M. Thompson and in particular to his *The French Revolution* (1943) and *Napoleon Bonaparte, his Rise and Fall* (1952). Prof. A. Goodwin's *The French Revolution* (1953) in the present series appeared too late for use.

Serious thinking on the general issues raised by the study of the period must begin with Alexis de Tocqueville's *L'Ancien Régime et la Révolution* published originally in 1856, of which a new edition appeared in 1952, in the complete Tocqueville now being edited by J. P. Mayer; Vol. I of A. Sorel, *L'Europe et la Révolution Française* (1885) remains the classic treatment of the international theme. Two recent books are fundamental: *Du Pouvoir* by Bertrand de Jouvenel (1945), published in an English translation as *Power* (1947), and J. L. Talmon, *The Origins of Totalitarian Democracy* (1952).

INDEX

harper ✦ torchbooks

† The New American Nation Series, edited by Henry Steele Commager and Richard B. Morris.
‡ American Perspectives series, edited by Bernard Wishy and William E. Leuchtenburg.
α History of Europe series, edited by J. H. Plumb.
§ The Library of Religion and Culture, edited by Benjamin Nelson.
‖ Researches in the Social, Cultural, and Behavioral Sciences, edited by Benjamin Nelson.
Σ Harper Modern Science Series, edited by James A. Newman.
° Not for sale in Canada.
+ Documentary History of the United States series, edited by Richard B. Morris.
# Documentary History of Western Civilization series, edited by Eugene C. Black and Leonard W. Levy.
Λ The Economic History of the United States series, edited by Henry David et al.
¶ European Perspectives series, edited by Eugene C. Black.
** Contemporary Essays series, edited by Leonard W. Levy.
* The Stratum Series, edited by John Hale.

PERRY MILLER: Errand Into the Wilderness
TB/1139
PERRY MILLER & T. H. JOHNSON, Eds.: The Puritans: *A Sourcebook of Their Writings*
Vol. I TB/1093; Vol. II TB/1094
EDMUND S. MORGAN: The Puritan Family: *Religion and Domestic Relations in Seventeenth Century New England* TB/1227
RICHARD B. MORRIS: Government and Labor in Early America TB/1244
WALLACE NOTESTEIN: The English People on the Eve of Colonization: 1603-1630. † *Illus.*
TB/3006
FRANCIS PARKMAN: The Seven Years War: *A Narrative Taken from Montcalm and Wolfe,* The Conspiracy of Pontiac, *and* A Half-Century of Conflict. *Edited by John H. McCallum* TB/3083
LOUIS B. WRIGHT: The Cultural Life of the American Colonies: 1607-1763. † *Illus.*
TB/3005
YVES F. ZOLTVANY, Ed.: The French Tradition in America + HR/1425

American Studies: The Revolution to 1860

JOHN R. ALDEN: The American Revolution: 1775-1783. † *Illus.* TB/3011
MAX BELOFF, Ed.: The Debate on the American Revolution, 1761-1783: *A Sourcebook*
TB/1225
RAY A. BILLINGTON: The Far Western Frontier: 1830-1860. † *Illus.* TB/3012
STUART BRUCHEY: The Roots of American Economic Growth, 1607-1861: *An Essay in Social Causation.* New Introduction by the Author.
TB/1350
WHITNEY R. CROSS: The Burned-Over District: *The Social and Intellectual History of Enthusiastic Religion in Western New York, 1800-1850* TB/1242
NOBLE E. CUNNINGHAM, JR., Ed.: The Early Republic, 1789-1828 + HR/1394
GEORGE DANGERFIELD: The Awakening of American Nationalism, 1815-1828. † *Illus.*
TB/3061
CLEMENT EATON: The Freedom-of-Thought Struggle in the Old South. *Revised and Enlarged. Illus.* TB/1150
CLEMENT EATON: The Growth of Southern Civilization, 1790-1860. † *Illus.* TB/3040
ROBERT H. FERRELL, Ed.: Foundations of American Diplomacy, 1775-1872 + HR/1393
LOUIS FILLER: The Crusade against Slavery: 1830-1860. † *Illus.* TB/3029
DAVID H. FISCHER: The Revolution of American Conservatism: *The Federalist Party in the Era of Jeffersonian Democracy* TB/1449
WILLIAM W. FREEHLING, Ed.: The Nullification Era: *A Documentary Record* ‡ TB/3079
WILLIM W. FREEHLING: Prelude to Civil War: *The Nullification Controversy in South Carolina, 1816-1836* TB/1359
PAUL W. GATES: The Farmer's Age: *Agriculture, 1815-1860* Δ TB/1398
FELIX GILBERT: The Beginnings of American Foreign Policy: *To the Farewell Address*
TB/1200
ALEXANDER HAMILTON: The Reports of Alexander Hamilton. ‡ *Edited by Jacob E. Cooke*
TB/3060
THOMAS JEFFERSON: Notes on the State of Virginia. ‡ *Edited by Thomas P. Abernethy*
TB/3052
FORREST MCDONALD, Ed.: Confederation and Constitution, 1781-1789 + HR/1396

BERNARD MAYO: Myths and Men: *Patrick Henry, George Washington, Thomas Jefferson*
TB/1108
JOHN C. MILLER: Alexander Hamilton and the Growth of the New Nation TB/3057
JOHN C. MILLER: The Federalist Era: 1789-1801. † *Illus.* TB/3027
RICHARD B. MORRIS, Ed.: Alexander Hamilton and the Founding of the Nation. New Introduction by the Editor TB/1448
RICHARD B. MORRIS: The American Revolution Reconsidered TB/1363
CURTIS P. NETTELS: The Emergence of a National Economy, 1775-1815 Δ TB/1438
DOUGLASS C. NORTH & ROBERT PAUL THOMAS, Eds.: *The Growth of the American Economy to 1860* + HR/1352
R. B. NYE: The Cultural Life of the New Nation: 1776-1830. † *Illus.* TB/3026
GILBERT OSOFSKY, Ed.: Puttin' On Ole Massa: *The Slave Narratives of Henry Bibb, William Wells Brown, and Solomon Northup* ‡
TB/1432
JAMES PARTON: The Presidency of Andrew Jackson. *From Volume III of the* Life of Andrew Jackson. Ed. with Intro. by Robert V. Remini TB/3080
FRANCIS S. PHILBRICK: The Rise of the West, 1754-1830. † *Illus.* TB/3067
MARSHALL SMELSER: The Democratic Republic, 1801-1815 † TB/1406
TIMOTHY L. SMITH: Revivalism and Social Reform: *American Protestantism on the Eve of the Civil War* TB/1229
JACK M. SOSIN, Ed.: The Opening of the West + HR/1424
GEORGE ROGERS TAYLOR: The Transportation Revolution, 1815-1860 Δ TB/1347
A. F. TYLER: Freedom's Ferment: *Phases of American Social History from the Revolution to the Outbreak of the Civil War. Illus.*
TB/1074
GLYNDON G. VAN DEUSEN: The Jacksonian Era: 1828-1848. † *Illus.* TB/3028
LOUIS B. WRIGHT: Culture on the Moving Frontier TB/1053

American Studies: The Civil War to 1900

W. R. BROCK: An American Crisis: *Congress and Reconstruction, 1865-67* ° TB/1283
T. C. COCHRAN & WILLIAM MILLER: The Age of Enterprise: *A Social History of Industrial America* TB/1054
W. A. DUNNING: Reconstruction, Political and Economic: 1865-1877 TB/1073
HAROLD U. FAULKNER: Politics, Reform and Expansion: 1890-1900. † *Illus.* TB/3020
GEORGE M. FREDRICKSON: The Inner Civil War: *Northern Intellectuals and the Crisis of the Union* TB/1358
JOHN A. GARRATY: The New Commonwealth, 1877-1890 † TB/1410
JOHN A. GARRATY, Ed.: The Transformation of American Society, 1870-1890 + HR/1395
WILLIAM R. HUTCHISON, Ed.: American Protestant Thought: *The Liberal Era* ‡ TB/1385
HELEN HUNT JACKSON: A Century of Dishonor: *The Early Crusade for Indian Reform.* † *Edited by Andrew F. Rolle* TB/3063
ALBERT D. KIRWAN: Revolt of the Rednecks: *Mississippi Politics, 1876-1925* TB/1199
WILLIAM G. MCLOUGHLIN, Ed.: The American Evangelicals, 1800-1900: An Anthology ‡
TB/1382
ARTHUR MANN: Yankee Reforms in the Urban Age: *Social Reform in Boston, 1800-1900*
TB/1247

2

ARNOLD M. PAUL: Conservative Crisis and the Rule of Law: *Attitudes of Bar and Bench, 1887-1895. New Introduction by Author*
TB/1415

JAMES S. PIKE: The Prostrate State: *South Carolina under Negro Government.* ‡ *Intro. by Robert F. Durden*
TB/3085

WHITELAW REID: After the War: *A Tour of the Southern States, 1865-1866.* ‡ *Edited by C. Vann Woodward*
TB/3066

FRED A. SHANNON: The Farmer's Last Frontier: *...Agriculture, 1860-1897*
TB/1348

VERNON LANE WHARTON: The Negro in Mississippi, 1865-1890
TB/1178

American Studies: The Twentieth Century

RICHARD M. ABRAMS, Ed.: The Issues of the Populist and Progressive Eras, 1892-1912 +
HR/1428

RAY STANNARD BAKER: Following the Color Line: *American Negro Citizenship in Progressive Era.* ‡ *Edited by Dewey W. Grantham, Jr. Illus.*
TB/3053

RANDOLPH S. BOURNE: War and the Intellectuals: *Collected Essays, 1915-1919.* ‡ *Edited by Carl Resek*
TB/3043

A. RUSSELL BUCHANAN: The United States and World War II. † *Illus.*
Vol. I TB/3044; Vol. II TB/3045

THOMAS C. COCHRAN: The American Business System: *A Historical Perspective, 1900-1955*
TB/1080

FOSTER RHEA DULLES: America's Rise to World Power: 1898-1954. † *Illus.*
TB/3021

JEAN-BAPTISTE DUROSELLE: From Wilson to Roosevelt: *Foreign Policy of the United States, 1913-1945. Trans. by Nancy Lyman Roelker*
TB/1370

HAROLD U. FAULKNER: The Decline of Laissez Faire, 1897-1917
TB/1397

JOHN D. HICKS: Republican Ascendancy: 1921-1933. † *Illus.*
TB/3041

ROBERT HUNTER: Poverty: *Social Conscience in the Progressive Era.* ‡ *Edited by Peter d'A. Jones*
TB/3065

WILLIAM E. LEUCHTENBURG. Franklin D. Roosevelt and the New Deal: 1932-1940. † *Illus.*
TB/3025

WILLIAM E. LEUCHTENBURG, Ed.: The New Deal: *A Documentary History* +
HR/1354

ARTHUR S. LINK: Woodrow Wilson and the Progressive Era: 1910-1917. † *Illus.*
TB/3023

BROADUS MITCHELL: Depression Decade: *From New Era through New Deal, 1929-1941* ∆
TB/1439

GEORGE E. MOWRY: The Era of Theodore Roosevelt and the Birth of Modern America: 1900-1912. † *Illus.*
TB/3022

WILLIAM PRESTON, JR.: Aliens and Dissenters: *Federal Suppression of Radicals, 1903-1933*
TB/1287

WALTER RAUSCHENBUSCH: Christianity and the Social Crisis. ‡ *Edited by Robert D. Cross*
TB/3059

GEORGE SOULE: Prosperity Decade: *From War to Depression, 1917-1929* ∆
TB/1349

GEORGE B. TINDALL, Ed.: A Populist Reader: *Selections from the Works of American Populist Leaders*
TB/3069

TWELVE SOUTHERNERS: I'll Take My Stand: *The South and the Agrarian Tradition. Intro. by Louis D. Rubin, Jr.; Biographical Essays by Virginia Rock*
TB/1072

Art, Art History, Aesthetics

CREIGHTON GILBERT, Ed.: Renaissance Art **
Illus.
TB/1465

EMILE MALE: The Gothic Image: *Religious Art in France of the Thirteenth Century.* § *190 illus.*
TB/344

MILLARD MEISS: Painting in Florence and Siena After the Black Death: *The Arts, Religion and Society in the Mid-Fourteenth Century. 169 illus.*
TB/1148

ERWIN PANOFSKY: Renaissance and Renascences in Western Art. *Illus.*
TB/1447

ERWIN PANOFSKY: Studies in Iconology: *Humanistic Themes in the Art of the Renaissance. 180 illus.*
TB/1077

JEAN SEZNEC: The Survival of the Pagan Gods: *The Mythological Tradition and Its Place in Renaissance Humanism and Art. 108 illus.*
TB/2004

OTTO VON SIMSON: The Gothic Cathedral: *Origins of Gothic Architecture and the Medieval Concept of Order. 58 illus.*
TB/2018

HEINRICH ZIMMER: Myths and Symbols in Indian Art and Civilization. *70 illus.*
TB/2005

Asian Studies

WOLFGANG FRANKE: China and the West: *The Cultural Encounter, 13th to 20th Centuries. Trans. by R. A. Wilson*
TB/1326

L. CARRINGTON GOODRICH: A Short History of the Chinese People. *Illus.*
TB/3015

DAN N. JACOBS, Ed.: The New Communist Manifesto and Related Documents. *3rd revised edn.*
TB/1078

DAN N. JACOBS & HANS H. BAERWALD, Eds.: Chinese Communism: *Selected Documents*
TB/3031

BENJAMIN I. SCHWARTZ: Chinese Communism and the Rise of Mao
TB/1308

BENJAMIN I. SCHWARTZ: In Search of Wealth and Power: *Yen Fu and the West*
TB/1422

Economics & Economic History

C. E. BLACK: The Dynamics of Modernization: *A Study in Comparative History*
TB/1321

STUART BRUCHEY: The Roots of American Economic Growth, 1607-1861: *An Essay in Social Causation. New Introduction by the Author.*
TB/1350

GILBERT BURCK & EDITORS OF *Fortune:* The Computer Age: *And its Potential for Management*
TB/1179

JOHN ELLIOTT CAIRNES: The Slave Power. ‡ *Edited with Introduction by Harold D. Woodman*
TB/1433

SHEPARD B. CLOUGH, THOMAS MOODIE & CAROL MOODIE, Eds.: Economic History of Europe: *Twentieth Century* #
HR/1388

THOMAS C. COCHRAN: The American Business System: *A Historical Perspective, 1900-1955*
TB/1180

ROBERT A. DAHL & CHARLES E. LINDBLOM: Politics, Economics, and Welfare: *Planning and Politico-Economic Systems Resolved into Basic Social Processes*
TB/3037

PETER F. DRUCKER: The New Society: *The Anatomy of Industrial Order*
TB/1082

HAROLD U. FAULKNER: The Decline of Laissez Faire, 1897-1917 ∆
TB/1397

PAUL W. GATES: The Farmer's Age: *Agriculture, 1815-1860* ∆
TB/1398

WILLIAM GREENLEAF, Ed.: American Economic Development Since 1860 +
HR/1353

J. L. & BARBARA HAMMOND: The Rise of Modern Industry. || *Introduction by R. M. Hartwell*
TB/1417

ROBERT L. HEILBRONER: The Future as History: *The Historic Currents of Our Time and the Direction in Which They Are Taking America* TB/1386
ROBERT L. HEILBRONER: The Great Ascent: *The Struggle for Economic Development in Our Time* TD/3030
FRANK H. KNIGHT: The Economic Organization TB/1214
DAVID S. LANDES: Bankers and Pashas: *International Finance and Economic Imperialism in Egypt. New Preface by the Author* TB/1412
ROBERT LATOUCHE: The Birth of Western Economy: *Economic Aspects of the Dark Ages* TB/1290
ABBA P. LERNER: Everybody's Business: *A Reexamination of Current Assumptions in Economics and Public Policy* TB/3051
W. ARTHUR LEWIS: Economic Survey, 1919-1939 TB/1446
W. ARTHUR LEWIS: The Principles of Economic Planning. *New Introduction by the Author°* TB/1436
ROBERT GREEN MC CLOSKEY: American Conservatism in the Age of Enterprise TB/1137
PAUL MANTOUX: The Industrial Revolution in the Eighteenth Century: *An Outline of the Beginnings of the Modern Factory System in England°* TB/1079
WILLIAM MILLER, Ed.: Men in Business: *Essays on the Historical Role of the Entrepreneur* TB/1081
GUNNAR MYRDAL: An International Economy. *New Introduction by the Author* TB/1445
HERBERT A. SIMON: The Shape of Automation: *For Men and Management* TB/1245
PERRIN STRYER: The Character of the Executive: *Eleven Studies in Managerial Qualities* TB/1041
RICHARD S. WECKSTEIN, Ed.: Expansion of World Trade and the Growth of National Economies ** TB/1373

Education

JACQUES BARZUN: The House of Intellect TB/1051
RICHARD M. JONES, Ed.: Contemporary Educational Psychology: *Selected Readings *** TB/1292
CLARK KERR: The Uses of the University TB/1264

Historiography and History of Ideas

HERSCHEL BAKER: The Image of Man: *A Study of the Idea of Human Dignity in Classical Antiquity, the Middle Ages, and the Renaissance* TB/1047
J. BRONOWSKI & BRUCE MAZLISH: The Western Intellectual Tradition: *From Leonardo to Hegel* TB/3001
EDMUND BURKE: On Revolution. Ed. by Robert A. Smith TB/1401
WILHELM DILTHEY: Pattern and Meaning in History: *Thoughts on History and Society.° Edited with an Intro. by H. P. Rickman* TB/1075
ALEXANDER GRAY: The Socialist Tradition: *Moses to Lenin °* TB/1375
J. H. HEXTER: More's Utopia: *The Biography of an Idea. Epilogue by the Author* TB/1195
H. STUART HUGHES: History as Art and as Science: *Twin Vistas on the Past* TB/1207
ARTHUR O. LOVEJOY: The Great Chain of Being: *A Study of the History of an Idea* TB/1009
JOSE ORTEGA Y GASSET: The Modern Theme. *Introduction by Jose Ferrater Mora* TB/1038

RICHARD H. POPKIN: The History of Scepticism from Erasmus to Descartes. *Revised Edition* TB/1391
G. J. RENIER: History: *Its Purpose and Method* TB/1209
MASSIMO SALVADORI, Ed.: Modern Socialism # HR/1374
GEORG SIMMEL et al.: Essays on Sociology, Philosophy and Aesthetics. *Edited by Kurt H. Wolff* TB/1234
BRUNO SNELL: The Discovery of the Mind: *The Greek Origins of European Thought* TB/1018
W. WARREN WAGER, ed.: European Intellectual History Since Darwin and Marx TB/1297
W. H. WALSH: Philosophy of History: *In Introduction* TB/1020

History: General

HANS KOHN: The Age of Nationalism: *The First Era of Global History* TB/1380
BERNARD LEWIS: The Arabs in History ° TB/1029
BERNARD LEWIS: The Middle East and the West ° TB/1274

History: Ancient

A. ANDREWS: The Greek Tyrants TB/1103
ERNST LUDWIG EHRLICH: A Concise History of Israel: *From the Earliest Times to the Destruction of the Temple in A.D. 70 °* TB/128
ADOLF ERMAN, Ed.: The Ancient Egyptians: *A Sourcebook of their Writings. New Introduction by William Kelly Simpson* TB/1233
THEODOR H. GASTER: Thespis: *Ritual Myth and Drama in the Ancient Near East* TB/1281
MICHAEL GRANT: Ancient History ° TB/1190
A. H. M. JONES, Ed.: A History of Rome through the Fifgth Century # *Vol. I: The Republic* HR/1364
Vol. II The Empire: HR/1460
SAMUEL NOAH KRAMER: Sumerian Mythology TB/1055
NAPHTALI LEWIS & MEYER REINHOLD, Eds.: Roman Civilization *Vol. I: The Republic* TB/1231
Vol. II: The Empire TB/1232

History: Medieval

MARSHALL W. BALDWIN, Ed.: Christianity Through the 13th Century # HR/1468
MARC BLOCH: Land and Work in Medieval Europe. *Translated by J. E. Anderson* TB/1452
HELEN CAM: England Before Elizabeth TB/1026
NORMAN COHN: The Pursuit of the Millennium: *Revolutionary Messianism in Medieval and Reformation Europe* TB/1037
G. G. COULTON: Medieval Village, Manor, and Monastery HR/1022
HEINRICH FICHTENAU: The Carolingian Empire: *The Age of Charlemagne. Translated with an Introduction by Peter Munz* TB/1142
GALBERT OF BRUGES: The Murder of Charles the Good: *A Contemporary Record of Revolutionary Change in 12th Century Flanders. Translated with an Introduction by James Bruce Ross* TB/1311
F. L. GANSHOF: Feudalism TB/1058
F. L. GANSHOF: The Middle Ages: *A History of International Relations. Translated by Rémy Hall* TB/1411
W. O. HASSALL, Ed.: Medieval England: *As Viewed by Contemporaries* TB/1205
DENYS HAY: The Medieval Centuries ° TB/1192
DAVID HERLIHY, Ed.: Medieval Culture and Society # HR/1340

4

EUGENE C. BLACK, Ed.: European Political History, 1815-1870: *Aspects of Liberalism* ¶ TB/1331

ASA BRIGGS: The Making of Modern England, 1783-1867: *The Age of Improvement* ° TB/1203

D. W. BROGAN: The Development of Modern France ° Vol. I: *From the Fall of the Empire to the Dreyfus Affair* TB/1184 Vol. II: *The Shadow of War, World War I, Between the Two Wars* TB/1185

ALAN BULLOCK: Hitler, A Study in Tyranny. ° *Revised Edition. Illus.* TB/1123

EDMUND BURKE: On Revolution. *Ed. by Robert A. Smith* TB/1401

E. R. CARR: International Relations Between the Two World Wars. 1919-1939 ° TB/1279

E. H. CARR: The Twenty Years' Crisis, 1919-1939: *An Introduction to the Study of International Relations* ° TB/1122

GORDON A. CRAIG: From Bismarck to Adenauer: *Aspects of German Statecraft. Revised Edition* TB/1171

LESTER G. CROCKER, Ed.: The Age of Enlightenment # HR/1423

DENIS DIDEROT: The Encyclopedia: *Selections. Edited and Translated with Introduction by Stephen Gendzier* TB/1299

JACQUES DROZ: Europe between Revolutions, 1815-1848. ° *a Trans. by Robert Baldick* TB/1346

JOHANN GOTTLIEB FICHTE: Addresses to the German Nation. *Ed. with Intro. by George A. Kelly* ¶ TB/1366

FRANKLIN L. FORD: Robe and Sword: *The Re-Louis XIV* TB/1217

ROBERT & ELBORG FORSTER, Eds.: European Society in the Eighteenth Century # HR/1404

C. C. GILLISPIE: Genesis and Geology: *The Decades before Darwin* § TB/51

ALBERT GOODWIN, Ed.: The European Nobility in the Enghteenth Century TB/1313

ALBERT GOODWIN: The French Revolution TB/1064

ALBERT GUERARD: France in the Classical Age: *The Life and Death of an Ideal* TB/1183

JOHN B. HALSTED, Ed.: Romanticism # HR/1387

J. H. HEXTER: Reappraisals in History: *New Views on History and Society in Early Modern Europe* ° TB/1100

STANLEY HOFFMANN et al.: In Search of France: *The Economy, Society and Political System In the Twentieth Century* TB/1219

H. STUART HUGHES: The Obstructed Path: *French Social Thought in the Years of Desperation* TB/1451

JOHAN HUIZINGA: Dutch Civilisation in the 17th Century and Other Essays TB/1453

LIONAL KOCHAN: The Struggle for Germany: 1914-45 TB/1304

HANS KOHN: The Mind of Germany: *The Education of a Nation* TB/1204

HANS KOHN, Ed.: The Mind of Modern Russia: *Historical and Political Thought of Russia's Great Age* TB/1065

WALTER LAQUEUR & GEORGE L. MOSSE, Eds.: Education and Social Structure in the 20th Century. ° *Volume 6 of the Journal of Contemporary History* TB/1339

WALTER LAQUEUR & GEORGE L. MOSSE, Ed.: International Fascism, 1920-1945. ° *Volume 1 of the Journal of Contemporary History* TB/1276

WALTER LAQUEUR & GEORGE L. MOSSE, Eds.: Literature and Politics in the 20th Century. ° *Volume 5 of the Journal of Contemporary History.* TB/1328

WALTER LAQUEUR & GEORGE L. MOSSE, Eds.: The New History: *Trends in Historical Research and Writing Since World War II.* ° *Volume 4 of the Journal of Contemporary History* TB/1327

WALTER LAQUEUR & GEORGE L. MOSSE, Eds.: 1914: *The Coming of the First World War.* ° *Volume3 of the Journal of Contemporary History* TB/1306

C. A. MACARTNEY, Ed.: The Habsburg and Hohenzollern Dynasties in the Seventeenth and Eighteenth Centuries # HR/1400

JOHN MCMANNERS: European History, 1789-1914: *Men, Machines and Freedom* TB/1419

PAUL MANTOUX: The Industrial Revolution in the Eighteenth Century: *An Outline of the Beginnings of the Modern Factory System in England* TB/1079

FRANK E. MANUEL: The Prophets of Paris: *Turgot, Condorcet, Saint-Simon, Fourier, and Comte* TB/1218

KINGSLEY MARTIN: French Liberal Thought in the Eighteenth Century: *A Study of Political Ideas from Bayle to Condorcet* TB/1114

NAPOLEON III: Napoleonic Ideas: *Des Idées Napoléoniennes, par le Prince Napoléon-Louis Bonaparte. Ed. by Brison D. Gooch* ¶ TB/1336

FRANZ NEUMANN: Behemoth: *The Structure and Practice of National Socialism, 1933-1944* TB/1289

DAVID OGG: Europe of the Ancien Régime, 1715-1783 ° *a* TB/1271

GEORGE RUDE: Revolutionary Europe, 1783-1815 ° *a* TB/1272

MASSIMO SALVADORI, Ed.: Modern Socialism # TB/1374

HUGH SETON-WATSON: Eastern Europe Between the Wars, 1918-1941 TB/1330

DENIS MACK SMITH, Ed.: The Making of Italy, 1796-1870 # HR/1356

ALBERT SOREL: Europe Under the Old Regime. *Translated by Francis H. Herrick* TB/1121

ROLAND N. STROMBERG, Ed.: Realism, Naturalism, and Symbolism: *Modes of Thought and Expression in Europe, 1848-1914* # HR/1355

A. J. P. TAYLOR: From Napoleon to Lenin: *Historical Essays* ° TB/1268

A. J. P. TAYLOR: The Habsburg Monarchy, 1809-1918: *A History of the Austrian Empire and Austria-Hungary* ° TB/1187

J. M. THOMPSON: European History, 1494-1789 TB/1431

DAVID THOMSON, Ed.: France: Empire and Republic, 1850-1940 # HR/1387

ALEXIS DE TOCQUEVILLE & GUSTAVE DE BEAUMONT: Tocqueville and Beaumont on Social Reform. *Ed. and trans. with Intro. by Seymour Drescher* TB/1343

G. M. TREVELYAN: British History in the Nineteenth Century and After: 1792-1919 ° TB/1251

H. R. TREVOR-ROPER: Historical Essays TB/1269

W. WARREN WAGAR, Ed.: Science, Faith, and MAN: *European Thought Since 1914* # HR/1362

MACK WALKER, Ed.: Metternich's Europe, 1813-1848 # HR/1361

ELIZABETH WISKEMANN: Europe of the Dictators, 1919-1945 ° *a* TB/1273

JOHN B. WOLF: France: 1814-1919: *The Rise of a Liberal-Democratic Society* TB/3019

Literature & Literary Criticism

JACQUES BARZUN: The House of Intellect TB/1051

W. J. BATE: From Classic to Romantic: *Premises of Taste in Eighteenth Century England* TB/1036
VAN WYCK BROOKS: Van Wyck Brooks: The Early Years: *A Selection from his Works, 1908-1921 Ed. with Intro. by Claire Sprague* TB/3082
ERNST R. CURTIUS: European Literature and the Latin Middle Ages. *Trans. by Willard Trask* TB/2015
RICHMOND LATTIMORE, Translator: The Odyssey of Homer TB/1389
JOHN STUART MILL: On Bentham and Coleridge. *Introduction by F. R. Leavis* TB/1070
SAMUEL PEPYS: The Diary of Samual Pepys. ° *Edited by O. F. Morshead. 60 illus. by Ernest Shepard* TB/1007
ROBERT PREYER, Ed.: Victorian Literature ** TB/1302
ALBION W. TOURGEE: A Fool's Errand: *A Novel of the South during Reconstruction. Intro. by George Fredrickson* TB/3074
BASIL WILEY: Nineteenth Century Studies: *Coleridge to Matthew Arnold* ° TB/1261
RAYMOND WILLIAMS: Culture and Society, 1780-1950 ° TB/1252

Philosophy

HENRI BERGSON: Time and Free Will: *An Essay on the Immediate Data of Consciousness* ° TB/1021
LUDWIG BINSWANGER: Being-in-the-World: *Selected Papers. Trans. with Intro. by Jacob Needleman* TB/1365
H. J. BLACKHAM: Six Existentialist Thinkers: *Kierkegaard, Nietzsche, Jaspers, Marcel, Heidegger, Sartre* ° TB/1002
J. M. BOCHENSKI: The Methods of Contemporary Thought. *Trans. by Peter Caws* TB/1377
CRANE BRINTON: Nietzsche. *Preface, Bibliography, and Epilogue by the Author* TB/1197
ERNST CASSIRER: Rousseau, Kant and Goethe. *Intro. by Peter Gay* TB/1092
FREDERICK COPLESTON, S. J.: Medieval Philosophy TB/376
F. M. CORNFORD: From Religion to Philosophy: *A Study in the Origins of Western Speculation* § TB/20
WILFRID DESAN: The Tragic Finale: *An Essay on the Philosophy of Jean-Paul Sartre* TB/1030
MARVIN FARBER: The Aims of Phenomenology: *The Motives, Methods, and Impact of Husserl's Thought* TB/1291
MARVIN FARBER: Basic Issues of Philosophy: *Experience, Reality, and Human Values* TB/1344
MARVIN FARBER: Phenomenology and Existence: *Towards a Philosophy within Nature* TB/1295
PAUL FRIEDLANDER: Plato: *An Introduction* TB/2017
MICHAEL GELVEN: A Commentary on Heidegger's "Being and Time" TB/1464
J. GLENN GRAY: Hegel and Greek Thought TB/1409
W. K. C. GUTHRIE: The Greek Philosophers: *From Thales to Aristotle* ° TB/1008
G. W. F. HEGEL: On Art, Religion Philosophy: *Introductory Lectures to the Realm of Absolute Spirit.* || *Edited with an Introduction by J. Glenn Gray* TB/1463
G. W. F. HEGEL: Phenomenology of Mind. ° || *Introduction by George Lichtheim* TB/1303
MARTIN HEIDEGGER: Discourse on Thinking. *Translated with a Preface by John M. Anderson and E. Hans Freund. Introduction by John M. Anderson* TB/1459

F. H. HEINEMANN: Existentialism and the Modern Predicament TB/28
WERER HEISENBERG: Physics and Philosophy: *The Revolution in Modern Science. Intro. by F. S. C. Northrop* TB/549
EDMUND HUSSERL: Phenomenology and the Crisis of Philosophy. § *Translated with an Introduction by Quentin Lauer* TB/1170
IMMANUEL KANT: Groundwork of the Metaphysic of Morals. *Translated and Analyzed by H. J. Paton* TB/1159
IMMANUEL KANT: Lectures on Ethics. § *Introduction by Lewis White Beck* TB/105
WALTER KAUFMANN, Ed.: Religion From Tolstoy to Camus: *Basic Writings on Religious Truth and Morals* TB/123
QUENTIN LAUER: Phenomenology: *Its Genesis and Prospect. Preface by Aron Gurwitsch* TB/1169
MAURICE MANDELBAUM: The Problem of Historical Knowledge: *An Answer to Relativism* TB/1338
GEORGE A. MORGAN: What Nietzsche Means TB/1198
H. J. PATON: The Categorical Imperative: *A Study in Kant's Moral Philosophy* TB/1325
MICHAEL POLANYI: Personal Knowledge: *Towards a Post-Critical Philosophy* TB/1158
KARL R. POPPER: Conjectures and Refutations: *The Growth of Scientific Knowledge* TB/1376
WILLARD VAN ORMAN QUINE: Elementary Logic *Revised Edition* TB/577
WILLARD VAN ORMAN QUINE: From a Logical Point of View: *Logico-Philosophical Essays* TB/566
JOHN E. SMITH: Themes in American Philosophy: *Purpose, Experience and Community* TB/1466
MORTON WHITE: Foundations of Historical Knowledge TB/1440
WILHELM WINDELBAND: A History of Philosophy *Vol. I: Greek, Roman, Medieval* TB/38 *Vol. II: Renaissance, Enlightenment, Modern* TB/39
LUDWIG WITTGENSTEIN: The Blue and Brown Books ° TB/1211
LUDWIG WITTGENSTEIN: Notebooks, 1914-1916 TB/1441

Political Science & Government

C. E. BLACK: The Dynamics of Modernization: *A Study in Comparative History* TB/1321
KENNETH E. BOULDING: Conflict and Defense: *A General Theory of Action* TB/3024
DENIS W. BROGAN: Politics in America. *New Introduction by the Author* TB/1469
CRANE BRINTON: English Political Thought in the Nineteenth Century TB/1071
ROBERT CONQUEST: Power and Policy in the USSR: *The Study of Soviet Dynastics* ° TB/1307
ROBERT A. DAHL & CHARLES E. LINDBLOM: Politics, Economics, and Welfare: *Planning and Politico-Economic Systems Resolved into Basic Social Processes* TB/1277
HANS KOHN: Political Ideologies of the 20th Century TB/1277
ROY C. MACRIDIS, Ed.: Political Parties: *Contemporary Trends and Ideas* ** TB/1322
ROBERT GREEN MC CLOSKEY: American Conservatism in the Age of Enterprise, 1865-1910 TB/1137
MARSILIUS OF PADUA: The Defender of Peace. *The Defensor Pacis. Translated with an Introduction by Alan Gewirth* TB/1310
KINGSLEY MARTIN: French Liberal Thought in the Eighteenth Century: *A Study of Political Ideas from Bayle to Condorcet* TB/1114

RUDOLF BULTMANN and KARL KUNDSIN: Form Criticism: *Two Essays on New Testament Research. Trans. by F. C. Grant*   TB/96
WILLIAM A. CLEBSCH & CHARLES R. JAEKLE: Pastoral Care in Historical Perspective: *An Essay with Exhibits*   TB/148
FREDERICK FERRE: Language, Logic and God. *New Preface by the Author*   TB/1407
LUDWIG FEUERBACH: The Essence of Christianity. § *Introduction by Karl Barth. Foreword by H. Richard Niebuhr*   TB/11
C. C. GILLISPIE: Genesis and Geology: *The Decades before Darwin* §   TB/51
ADOLF HARNACK: What Is Christianity? § *Introduction by Rudolf Bultmann*   TB/17
KYLE HASELDEN: The Racial Problem in Christian Perspective   TB/116
MARTIN HEIDEGGER: Discourse on Thinking. *Translated with a Preface by John M. Anderson and E. Hans Freund. Introduction by John M. Anderson*   TB/1459
IMMANUEL KANT: Religion Within the Limits of Reason Alone. § *Introduction by Theodore M. Greene and John Silber*   TB/FG
WALTER KAUFMANN, Ed.: Religion from Tolstoy to Camus: *Basic Writings on Religious Truth and Morals. Enlarged Edition*   TB/123
JOHN MACQUARRIE: An Existentialist Theology: *A Comparison of Heidegger and Bultmann.* ° *Foreword by Rudolf Bultmann*   TB/125
H. RICHARD NIERUHR: Christ and Culture   TB/3
H. RICHARD NIEBUHR: The Kingdom of God in America   TB/49
ANDERS NYGREN: Agape and Eros. *Translated by Philip S. Watson* °   TB/1430
JOHN H. RANDALL, JR.: The Meaning of Religion for Man. *Revised with New Intro. by the Author*   TB/1379
WALTER RAUSCHENBUSCHS Christianity and the Social Crisis. ‡ *Edited by Robert D. Cross*   TB/3059
JOACHIM WACH: Understanding and Believing. *Ed. with Intro. by Joseph M. Kitagawa*   TB/1399

Science and Mathematics

JOHN TYLER BONNER: The Ideas of Biology. Σ *Illus.*   TB/570
W. E. LE GROS CLARK: The Antecedents of Man: *An Introduction to the Evolution of the Primates.* ° *Illus.*   TB/559
ROBERT E. COKER: Streams, Lakes, Ponds. *Illus.*   TB/586
ROBERT E. COKER: This Great and Wide Sea: *An Introduction to Oceanography and Marine Biology. Illus.*   TB/551
W. H. DOWDESWELL: Animal Ecology. *61 illus.*   TB/543
C. V. DURELL: Readable Relativity. *Foreword by Freeman J. Dyson*   TB/530
GEORGE GAMOW: Biography of Physics. Σ *Illus.*   TB/567
F. K. HARE: The Restless Atmosphere   TB/560
S. KORNER: The Philosophy of Mathematics: *An Introduction*   TB/547
J. R. PIERCE: Symbols, Signals and Noise: *The Nature and Process of Communication* Σ   TB/574
WILLARD VAN ORMAN QUINE: Mathematical Logic   TB/558

Science: History

MARIE BOAS: The Scientific Renaissance, 1450-1630 °   TB/583
W. DAMPIER, Ed.: Readings in the Literature of Science. *Illus.*   TB/512

STEPHEN TOULMIN & JUNE GOODFIELD: The Architecture of Matter: *The Physics, Chemistry and Physiology of Matter, Both Animate and Inanimate, as it has Evolved since the Beginnings of Science*   TB/584
STEPHEN TOULMIN & JUNE GOODFIELD: The Discovery of Time   TB/585
STEPHEN TOULMIN & JUNE GOODFIELD: The Fabric of the Heavens: *The Development of Astronomy and Dynamics*   TB/579

Science: Philosophy

J. M. BOCHENSKI: The Methods of Contemporary Thought. *Tr. by Peter Caws*   TB/1377
J. BRONOWSKI: Science and Human Values. *Revised and Enlarged. Illus.*   TB/505
WERNER HEISENBERG: Physics and Philosophy: *The Revolution in Modern Science. Introduction by F. S. C. Northrop*   TB/549
KARL R. POPPER: Conjectures and Refutations: *The Growth of Scientific Knowledge*   TB/1376
KARL R. POPPER: The Logic of Scientific Discovery   TB/576
STEPHEN TOULMIN: Foresight and Understanding: *An Enquiry into the Aims of Science. Foreword by Jacques Barzun*   TB/564
STEPHEN TOULMIN: The Philosophy of Science: *An Introduction*   TB/513

Sociology and Anthropology

REINHARD BENDIX: Work and Authority in Industry: *Ideologies of Management in the Course of Industrialization*   TB/3035
BERNARD BERELSON, Ed., The Behavioral Sciences Today   TB/1127
JOSEPH B. CASAGRANDE, Ed.: In the Company of Man: *Twenty Portraits of Anthropological Informants. Illus.*   TB/3047
KENNETH B. CLARK: Dark Ghetto: *Dilemmas of Social Power. Foreword by Gunnar Myrdal*   TB/1317
KENNETH CLARK & JEANNETTE HOPKINS: A Relevant War Against Poverty: *A Study of Community Action Programs and Observable Social Change*   TB/1480
W. E. LE GROS CLARK: The Antecedents of Man: *An Introduction to the Evolution of the Primates.* ° *Illus.*   TB/559
LEWIS COSER, Ed.: Political Sociology   TB/1293
ROSE L. COSER, Ed.: Life Cycle and Achievement in America **   TB/1434
ALLISON DAVIS & JOHN DOLLARD: Children of Bondage: *The Personality Development of Negro Youth in the Urban South* ‖   TB/3049
ST. CLAIR DRAKE & HORACE R. CAYTON: Black Metropolis: *A Study of Negro Life in a Northern City. Introduction by Everett C. Hughes. Tables, maps, charts, and graphs* Vol. I TB/1086; Vol. II TB/1087
PETER E. DRUCKER: The New Society: *The Anatomy of Industrial Order*   TB/1082
CORA DU BOIS: The People of Alor. *With a Preface by the Author* Vol. I *Illus.* TB/1042; Vol. II TB/1043
EMILE DURKHEIM et al.: Essays on Sociology and Philosophy: *with Appraisals of Durkheim's Life and Thought.* ‖ *Edited by Kurt H. Wolff*   TB/1151
LEON FESTINGER, HENRY W. RIECKEN, STANLEY SCHACHTER: When Prophecy Fails: *A Social and Psychological Study of a Modern Group that Predicted the Destruction of the World* ‖   TB/1132